$35.00   ¼05

HISTORY OF INVENTION

MEDICINE

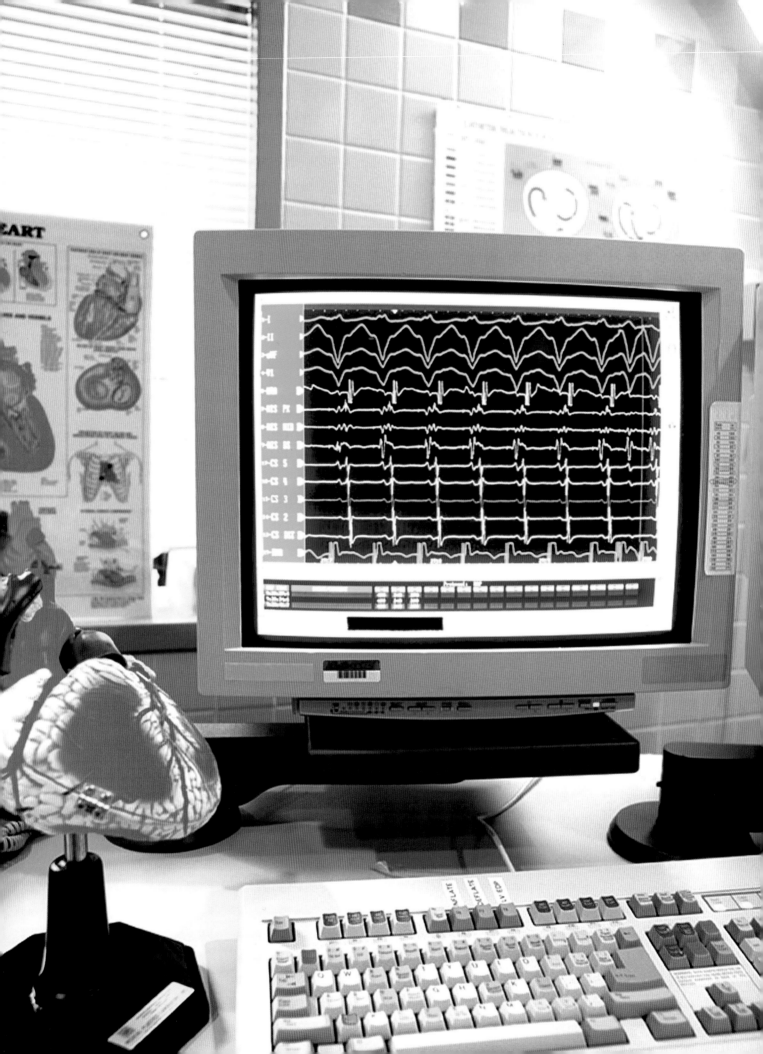

HISTORY OF INVENTION

MEDICINE

Daniel Gilpin

Facts On File, Inc.

Facts On File, Inc.
132 West 31st Street
New York, NY 10001

Library of Congress Cataloging-in-Publication Data

Daniel, Gilpin
   Medicine / Daniel Gilpin
      p. cm.
   Summary: Reviews the development of medicine and medical technology from the dawn of civilization to the present, including instruments, diagnostic tools, medicines, and alternative care.
   Includes bibliographical references and index.
   ISBN 0-8160-5442-8
   1. Medicine—History—Juvenile literature. [1. Medicine—History.] I. Title.

R133.5.G53 2004
610′ .9—dc22

                                    2003013453

Facts On File books are available at special discounts when purchased in bulk quantities for businesses, associations, institutions, or sales promotions. Please call our Special Sales Department in New York at (212) 967-8800 or (800) 322-8755.

You can find Facts On File on the World Wide Web at http://www.factsonfile.com

For The Brown Reference Group plc:
Project Editor: Tom Jackson
Design: Bradbury and Williams
Picture Research: Becky Cox
Managing Editor: Bridget Giles
Consultant: Dr. Kathleen Jones, Assistant Professor of History, Virginia Tech, Blacksburg, Virginia.

Printed and bound in Singapore

10 9 8 7 6 5 4 3 2 1

CONTENTS

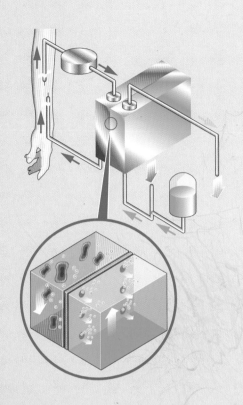

THE EARLY DAYS

It is hard to imagine now but there was once a time without doctors. When people became ill, they had only their body's own defenses to rely on. When that failed, they weakened and died.

Life before organized medicine was difficult and short. Many diseases that are now viewed as nonserious, such as influenza, might prove to be killers.

Minor accidents could also be as fatal as any disease. Without any way to close or clean wounds, even a cut could spell disaster. Infection might set in, and in many cases this led to blood poisoning or gangrene. Gangrene is a deadly condition, and without the benefits of modern drugs it generally results in death.

EARLY MEDICINE

The earliest forms of medicine were healing plants that grew naturally in the wild. When a person felt ill, they sought out the plants and ate some of them in the hope of soon feeling better. Wild chimpanzees in east Africa practice this behavior, searching for the leaves of a plant called *Aspilia* when they are unwell. It seems likely that our own

Romans did not wash in their homes. Instead they visited public baths such as this one in London from the 2nd century c.e. Romans did not use soap. They rubbed oil over their bodies and then scraped it off. This process removed any dirt and dead skin.

ancestors had similar habits. Aspilia itself is a popular natural remedy used by many people in central Africa to this day.

A disease that did not respond to treatment with plants might then be tackled with religion. People thought that illness was caused by demons inside the body. Shamans and other wise people performed rites to drive the evil spirits out of the sufferer's body. If the patient then recovered naturally, the magic was believed to have

Gods and Health

Before medicine was understood scientifically, sickness and disease were thought to have been caused by malevolent spirits or sent by the gods of enemies. In order to battle them, people turned to their own gods or magic cures provided by witches or shamans (above, in Sierra Leone). Witches and wizards are often thought of as being evil people. But a thousand years ago, they were the health workers of Europe. They made medicines from plants and animals, which were swallowed or applied directly to the affected area.

Many people had their own gods of healing. The ancient Greeks offered sacrifices to Asclepius, the son of Apollo. In many cultures, a belief in a god is still trusted to cure illness. Devout Christians and Hindus, for example, travel to holy sites to pray for a cure. In Haiti, voodoo is a religion that has grown from a fusion of Christianity and African beliefs in spirits. These spirits play a role in all areas of people's lives, including illness. Voodoo priests and priestesses drive out disease-causing spirits from the body.

worked. Shamans often used plant preparations during their rituals, which might also have helped.

The first evidence of modern medical practices similar to those used today comes from the remains of people who died thousands of years ago. Skeletons of people from this time have been found with breaks that healed far more cleanly than they could have done naturally. Archaeologists think that the bones were set with splints. Skeletons have been found buried with the splints still intact.

THE FIRST DOCTORS

The first writing system appeared in Mesopotamia (modern Iraq) around 3300 B.C.E. Among other things, writing was used to record medical techniques. From these early medical textbooks, we know that Mesopotamian doctors were trained to wash and bandage wounds, lance boils, and make a variety of ointments.

Around 1770 B.C.E., the *Code of Hammurabi* was written, outlining the laws of the Mesopotamian region. Of the 282 laws written down, 17 related to doctors and medical practice. One gave the amounts surgeons could charge for successful operations: "Ten silver shekels for a nobleman, five for a commissioner, and two for a slave." Another listed the punishments for malpractice or failure. Some of these were extremely harsh. One, for example, stated that "if a doctor

performed an operation and caused a lord's death...they shall cut off his hand."

Soon after writing appeared in Mesopotamia, the practice spread to Egypt. Egyptian hieroglyphs record the world's first named doctor, Sekhet'eanach. Like the techniques practiced in

A statue of Sekmet, the Egyptian lion goddess. Sekmet was the goddess of surgeons. Her priests were also doctors.

Trepanning

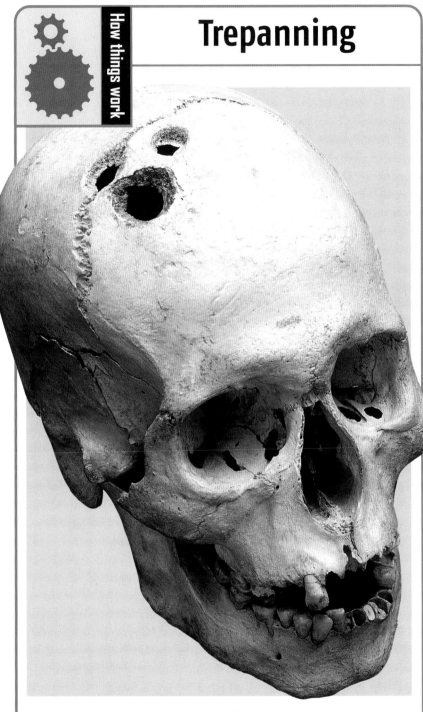

People have taken potions and other remedies for ailments since before the beginning of history, and it seems likely that they undertook some basic surgery, too. One surgical operation for which there is definite prehistoric evidence is trepanning, a procedure in which a hole was cut in the skull (above). Trepanning was probably an attempt to cure migraines by releasing evil spirits. Trepanned skulls are known that date back more than 10,000 years and have been found in most parts of the world. Evidence of bone healing around the holes shows that many patients survived the operation.

Mesopotamia, Egyptian medicine was part science and part religion. Patients and doctors alike believed in the power of gods to intervene and change the course of an illness. While treatments were being given, spells and chants were often read out or ceremonies were performed. These activities were meant to make contact with gods and ask for their help. Many Egyptians wore charms to protect themselves from diseases.

Egyptian medical knowledge was stored in volumes known as the *Books of Thoth*. Thoth was the ancient Egyptian god of wisdom, and these books were kept by priests in temples dedicated to him. None of the *Books of Thoth* now survive, but a medical book from around 1500 B.C.E. has been found that is thought to have been based on them. It lists treatments for a wide variety of ailments and illnesses. Among these are instructions on how to remove cysts and tumors, as well as procedures to relieve chest complaints. The ancient Egyptians applied willow extracts to wounds to prevent infection. They also used yeast to treat leg ulcers. Both of these procedures have since been shown to work by modern doctors. Many other ancient remedies did not work, but these were destined to be forgotten. Egyptian medicine progressed by trial and error, and some of the treatments that were developed thousands of years ago are still used today.

Egyptian Medicine

Ancient Egypt was the earliest known civilization to have its own specialized medical profession. The first of its doctors to be recorded by name was a man called Sekhet'eanach. Hieroglyphs dated to around 3000 B.C.E. tell how he healed the pharaoh's nostrils. This is probably a reference to him unblocking congestion caused by flu or a cold.

Egypt's greatest doctor, Imhotep (right), lived around 2600 B.C.E. Chief advisor and physician to King Zozer, he is perhaps better known for his role in the design of the first Egyptian pyramid. Just over 200 years after his death, Imhotep was made a god of healing and great temples were erected in his honor.

In life, Imhotep played the dual roles of physician and priest. Egyptian medicine was bound up with religion. Different gods were believed to control different parts of the body. Herbal remedies and treatments made from animal parts were used with spells.

The herbs used included thyme to dull pain, and aloe vera, which was used to treat worms. Honey was applied to cuts to prevent infection. This was probably a very successful treatment, as honey is known to have germ-killing properties.

The ancient Egyptians are famous for their skill in preserving the dead as mummies, but they also performed surgery on the living. Wounds were classified into one of three categories: Those that could be treated, those that could be contended with, and those that could not be treated. Wounds that could be contended with were considered too dangerous to treat until the patient had begun to rally and recovered some strength. Surgical equipment was similar to that used today. Egyptian surgeons had scalpels (knives), saws, drills, hooks and forceps (large tongs) at their disposal. These tools and others are displayed in hieroglyphs on the outer wall of the temple of Kom Ombo beside the Nile River in southern Egypt.

Mending Breaks

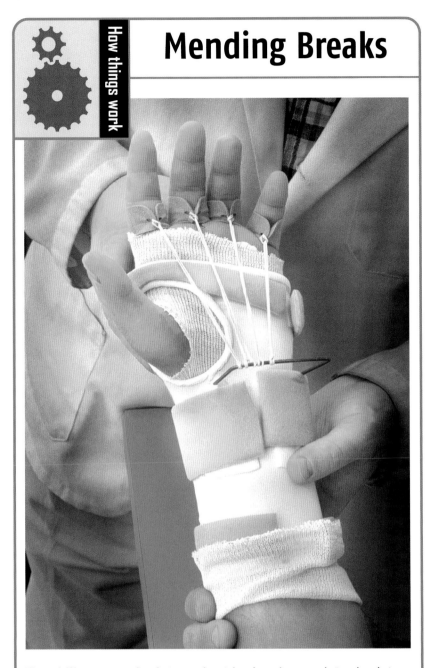

The ability to manipulate and set broken bones dates back to long before the advent of modern medicine. Many ancient skeletons have been found by archaeologists with evidence of serious breaks that have been corrected and healed.

Today, a broken arm or leg, once realigned, is encased in plaster of Paris or held firm in a plastic brace (above). In the past, straight objects called splints were strapped to the broken limb to hold the bones in place while they healed.

Excavation of a Pueblo burial site in New Mexico has shown that Native American people used splints. The skeleton of one young woman, who had several injuries from a serious accident, was found with six artfully carved wooden splints around the fractured bones of her forearm.

By 1200 B.C.E., the Israelites also had a good understanding of medicine. Records tell us that they were the first people to use quarantine (isolation) to prevent diseases from spreading. People with infectious illnesses were kept in their homes and not allowed to meet with others. After the disease had passed, the houses of infected people were scrubbed clean to ensure the illness did not return.

A NEW APPROACH

Modern medicine is often said to have begun with the ancient Greeks. Hippocrates (460–377 B.C.E) was the first doctor to practice medicine as a science without reference to gods. He is regarded as the father of modern medicine.

Like the Israelites, the ancient Greeks realized the importance of personal hygiene. The physician Diocles (240–180 B.C.E.), for example, recommended washing the body with clean water daily and even wrote of the benefits of peppermint powder for keeping teeth clean.

At around the same time as the Greeks were developing their new philosophy of medicine, people in India were also making important breakthroughs. It was here that the world's first hospitals appeared. Buddha (563-483 B.C.E.) preached the importance of caring for the sick, and his followers built wards for that purpose in monasteries. After Buddha's death, Buddhist kings created hospitals in many parts of the region.

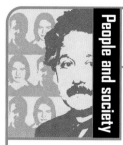

People and society

Hippocrates and Galen

The world's most famous doctor, even today, Hippocrates (right) lived and practiced 2,400 years ago. An ancient Greek, he spent his life on the island of Cos, where he put forward many new ideas about medicine and the treatment of disease. Unlike his predecessors, Hippocrates refused to explain illness as acts of the gods. He was the first person to describe medicine as a science rather than a religion.

Hippocrates' ideas about illness were often completely wrong. He believed that the body had four so-called *humors*—black bile, yellow bile, blood, and phlegm. Sickness was the result of imbalance between the humors. But he also stressed the importance of good diet, fresh air, and exercise to help the body with healing. And he was the first to emphasize the pattern of observation, diagnosis, treatment, and prognosis (predicted outcome) that is still followed by doctors even today.

Hippocrates' greatest legacy was his oath, which outlined medical ethics. All of his students had to swear to maintain patient confidentiality and never deliberately harm anyone in their care. New doctors still take the Hippocratic Oath today. Although many of his theories have been proved false, and his teachings forgotten, the father of medicine lives on in his code of conduct.

After Hippocrates, the Roman Galen is the most celebrated of all the ancient physicians. Born in Pergamum (now in modern Turkey) to a noble family, he became a doctor and was known for treating wounded gladiators. Years later, he became physician to the Roman emperor Marcus Aurelius.

Galen (above) significantly increased the understanding of anatomy by making many experiments on living animals and internal examinations of dead people. Although many of his conclusions were incorrect, he was the first person to introduce the concept of experimentation into medicine, and went on to influence medical practice in Europe for the next 1,400 years.

In Roman times (275 B.C.E–476 C.E.) medicine built on the principles established in ancient Greece. Through his studies, the Roman Galen (130-210 C.E.) brought a new understanding of human anatomy. Public baths, a great Roman invention, also made keeping clean a social event.

The Romans exported their knowledge to new places as their empire expanded. As the influence of Rome declined, however, most of that medical knowledge was lost. Many people returned to doing things the way that they had been done before.

REVISITED AND REBORN

Medical knowledge in Europe remained stagnant for a thousand years. However, Muslim doctors, such as Ibn Sina (980–1037), in the Middle East continued to build on medical knowledge from Greece, Rome, and South Asia.

It was not until the Renaissance that things began to change in Europe. In this period of history, knowledge of all types, including medical understanding, was "rediscovered" from ancient times. In 1543, Flemish scientist Andreas Vesalius (1514–64) published a book called *On the Fabric of the Human Body*. In it, he corrected mistakes made by Galen centuries before. Vesalius's work advanced the understanding of anatomy and became a standard textbook in medical schools. One mistake that Vesalius did not challenge was Galen's view on the movement of blood. The Roman doctor had said tiny holes allowed blood to flow from one side of the heart to the other. However, Vesalius could not find these holes. The misconception was cleared up in 1559 by the Italian anatomist Realdo Columbo (1516–59). He demonstrated that blood traveled between the two halves of the heart via the lungs.

Columbo's finding helped lead the English doctor William Harvey (1578–1657) to the greatest medical discovery of the 17th century. Harvey realized that the heart was a four-chambered pump and figured out how it drove blood around the body through its network of arteries and veins. In 1661, the Italian Marcello Malpighi (1628–94) found smaller blood vessels, called capillaries, which completed the blood circulation system. While these revelations did little to help people who were sick at the time, they did launch a new era of discovery, which changed medicine forever.

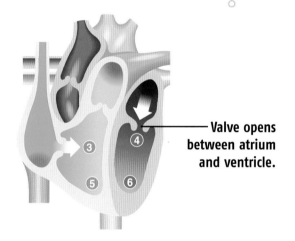

This diagram shows how the heart pumps blood to the lungs and around the body. This was first figured out by William Harvey in the 17th century.

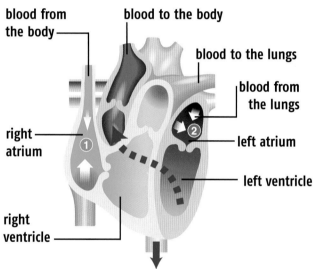

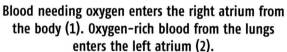

Blood needing oxygen enters the right atrium from the body (1). Oxygen-rich blood from the lungs enters the left atrium (2).

The atria contract to pump the blood into the ventricles (3 and 4). At the same time, the muscular walls of the ventricles relax to help blood enter (5 and 6).

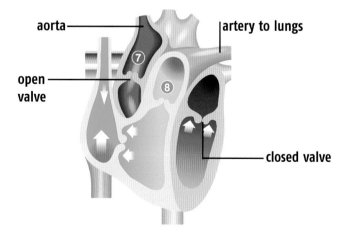

Valves open in the aorta and main artery to the lungs (7 and 8). Valves between the atria and ventricles close to keep blood flowing in the right direction.

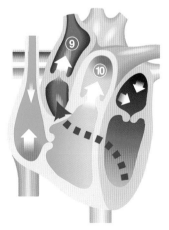

The left ventricle pumps oxygen-rich blood into the aorta (9), and the right ventricle sends oxygen-poor blood to the lungs (10), while the atria fill up with blood again.

Plague and Pestilence

Many diseases that today are rare or easily treated were widespread and incurable only a few hundred years ago. Poor sanitation and ignorance about the causes of illness meant that outbreaks of disease often flared up into epidemics. An epidemic is an outbreak of disease in which a large number of people are suffering from it at the same time.

Among the biggest killers were tuberculosis, typhoid, and cholera. We now know that all of these are caused by bacteria passed on either by coughing or in contaminated food and water. They can be prevented from spreading by applying simple rules of hygiene, such as covering the mouth when coughing or keeping drinking water and sewage separate. Back then, however, these seemingly obvious facts had yet to be discovered.

The most infamous disease of all was the bubonic plague, or Black Death. Passed on by bites from rat fleas, it killed one third of all Europeans, when it spread from Asia in the 14th century. Unlike typhoid and cholera, the Black Death was not just a disease of crowded cities (above), it affected people in the countryside as well. The nursery rhyme *Ring Around the Rosy* refers to the illness. The "ring around the rosy" was the red marks that appeared on the skin as plague set in. The "pocket full of posies" were herb pouches people carried to ward off the disease.

> ✱ **Fact** An epidemic that spreads around the world is called a pandemic. Doctors that study epidemics are known as epidemiologists.

THE FIRST HOSPITALS

A 15th-century drawing shows a ward in the Hôtel-Dieu hospital in Paris, France. This hospital was built in the 7th century. It is still open today and is the longest-running hospital in the world.

Hospitals are places that are designed to treat the sick and wounded. They are not as ancient as you might imagine. While the Egyptians and Greeks had temples to the gods of healing, they did not have hospitals. The sick received treatment at home, generally from their family.

The first hospitals were built in India around 500 B.C.E. By the reign of King Asoka (273–32 B.C.E.), Indian hospitals began to resemble modern ones. For example, they were kept very clean and had special areas where operations were performed.

Hospitals did not appear outside of Asia until the rise of the Roman Empire. From around 100 B.C.E., Roman hospitals were set up to care for soldiers. Each Roman legion had medical orderlies, or *medici*. The medici treated the soldiers' worst injuries in tents close to the battlefield.

The survivors were sent to forts along the frontier. Each fort had a hospital building, kept stocked with surgical instruments, medicines, and other supplies. The word *hospital* comes from the Latin word *hospitalis,* which means "guest house."

In 335 C.E., the Roman Emperor Constantine became a Christian. He ordered the closure of all *Aesculapia*, the temples to the Roman god of healing. Thirty years later, wealthy Christians began building the first hospitals for the sick and the poor.

16

In the 7th century, the new religion of Islam was spreading across Asia and Africa. In keeping with Islamic teachings many people started caring for the sick. This led to a very advanced hospital system. New institutions, inspired largely by the Persian Hospital in Djoundisabour (in modern Turkey), soon outnumbered the Roman military and Christian hospitals put together. The greatest Islamic hospitals built were in Damascus, Syria; Cairo, Egypt; and Baghdad, Iraq. Mental hospitals were also set up, centuries before they appeared in Europe.

Patients in Islamic hospitals were separated according to the state of their illness.

> *An Islamic painting shows a doctor visiting a patient. Medical knowledge from Rome and Greece was remembered in the Middle East after being forgotten in Europe.*

People in recovery were kept apart from the very sick, and provisions were made for those able to get up and walk around. There were even separate wards for different types of disease, such as eye conditions, diarrhea, fever, and gynecological disorders.

Medical schools were attached to many hospitals, with students taught using clinical reports collected from previous patients. Islamic doctors were the first to establish chemistry and pharmacology (the preparation of medicines) as sciences.

As Islam spread, Christian nations launched crusades, or religious wars, to regain lost territory. Christians returning from these wars brought money and knowledge with them, which they used to set up hospitals similar to Islamic ones. For example, in 1123, St. Bartholomew's Hospital was established in London.

The first American hospitals were built by European settlers. The earliest reference to the building of a hospital in North America dates from January 1494, when Columbus visited the island of Hispaniola (now divided into Haiti and the Dominican Republic). The first hospital in North America was built in Quebec, Canada in 1639. Philadelphia Hospital was set up in 1751 and is the oldest U.S. hospital.

SCIENTIFIC METHODS

Robert Koch looks at bacteria through a microscope. Koch became famous for discovering what microorganisms caused many diseases, such as tuberculosis, also known as consumption.

By the middle of the 17th century, the Renaissance, a period of rediscovery of knowledge in Europe, was drawing to a close. The modern world began to emerge with a new spirit of scientific enquiry. Where once the workings of the world had been ascribed to God, now logical explanations began to appear as new technologies were developed, and great thinkers put their minds to difficult questions.

This spirit of enquiry advanced all of the sciences and discoveries were spread from one discipline to another. The invention of the microscope led to developments in microbiology. This in turn had a huge impact on the science of medicine. In the 19th century, French biologist Louis Pasteur (1822–95) demonstrated that microorganisms could cause disease as part of his "germ" theory. Pasteur's work was taken a step further by the German microbiologist Robert Koch (1843–1910). Koch showed that a type of bacteria (tiny single-celled organisms) caused anthrax. Anthrax is a disease of cattle that can also kill people. It was the first illness to have its cause correctly identified. In 1876, when his proof was published, Koch became world famous. In 1880, he went on to discover the bacterium that causes tuberculosis, a deadly lung disease. Three years later, he identified the bacterium that causes cholera, a disease of the intestine which was very common at the time.

As his understanding of these bacteria, grew, Robert Koch formulated ways for the control of epidemics of cholera, such as keeping sewage away from drinking water and food. In 1893, his ideas were recognized by the medical community, and the methods he recommended still form the basis of cholera control.

FINDING THE CAUSE
Louis Pasteur also achieved great things toward the end of the 19th century. After hearing of Koch's success in identifying the cause of anthrax, Pasteur decided to try to find a way to prevent the disease.

How things work

Germ Theory

The idea that germs cause disease seems obvious to us today. Just 200 years ago, however, it was something that nobody knew. Sickness was blamed on everything from bad air and the climate to sin.

Although the germ theory of disease was a 19th-century development, ideas behind it date back to the end of the Renaissance. Hungarian doctor Ignaz Semmelweis (1818–1865), for example, noticed that when doctors washed their hands before delivering a baby, the new mother was unlikely to develop the deadly "childbirth fever." Although Semmelweis never knew it, this fever was actually transmitted by doctors delivering babies without washing after performing surgery.

In 1670, Dutch lens grinder Anton van Leeuwenhoek (1632–1723) first observed living microorganisms, or germs, through a home-made microscope. This began the science of microbiology, the study of life at the microscopic level. Although van Leeuwenhoek had seen bacteria and other microorganisms, they were explained away with the theory of spontaneous generation. This stated that living things arose spontaneously from non-living matter and frequently did so.

The first person to disprove this theory was Louis Pasteur. Pasteur had discovered that fermentation, the process used to make alcoholic drinks, was caused by microscopic yeast. In 1865, he was asked to find out why valuable silkworm caterpillars were being destroyed by disease. He demonstrated that the disease was caused by a microorganism that spread from one silk worm to another. This proved that the germ did not just appear spontaneously. He also explored how bacteria made food and drink spoil. He placed a sterile broth in a sealed flask (a model, above). He demonstrated that the broth stayed fresh until the glass seal was broken. Bacteria in the air then entered the flask and began to grow in the broth, making it go bad. Pasteur's discovery changed the way people practiced medicine and keeping things clean and sterilized became much more important.

Vaccination

Many of the world's worst diseases have been controlled or even wiped out by vaccinating people against them. Vaccination is achieved by giving people a small dose of the microorganism that causes the illness, called a pathogen. The dose has been made safe, either by killing the pathogen with heat, or by using weak strains. When the immune system detects the pathogen, it produces antibodies against it. These remain in the body and are there to fight active forms of the illness should the person become infected with the disease in the future.

The idea behind vaccination is not a new one. Serum made from smallpox pus was used in Turkey and across Asia since ancient times. However, this was a very risky business, and treatments often caused the disease, not prevent it. At the end of the 18th century, smallpox had become a dangerous problem in Britain. The disease was least common on the dairy farms in the west of England. A farmer called Benjamin Jesty living there slowly worked out why. He noticed that dairy workers who had already been infected with cowpox, a less dangerous disease caught from cattle, never contracted smallpox. In 1774, Jesty injected his family with a small amount of cowpox serum to immunize them. The news of their immunity eventually reached a doctor named Edward Jenner (1749–1823), who decided to study the phenomenon further. In 1796, Jenner injected an eight-year-old boy called James Phipps with cowpox, then, six weeks later, with smallpox. Fortunately, the boy never developed the deadly disease, and Jenner used the newly-tested vaccine to immunize hundreds of other people.

Immune Response

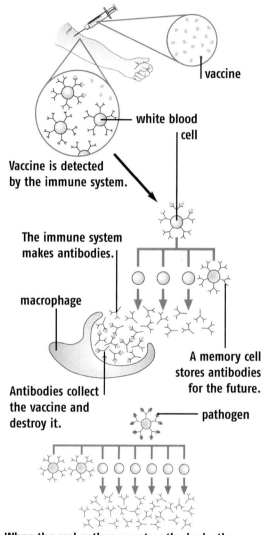

vaccine

white blood cell

Vaccine is detected by the immune system.

The immune system makes antibodies.

macrophage

Antibodies collect the vaccine and destroy it.

A memory cell stores antibodies for the future.

pathogen

When the real pathogen enters the body, the memory cells release the antibodies, which prevent the disease from taking hold.

Now that the bacteria had been discovered, he thought that he might be able to protect animals from it with a vaccine.

A vaccine is a drug that stops a person catching a certain disease.

At that point, the only disease with a successful vaccine was smallpox. Smallpox was prevented by injecting people with a serum containing the cowpox bacterium, *Vaccinia*. The word *vaccine* comes from this name. Pasteur wondered whether it was possible to vaccinate by using the same bacteria that caused a disease. In 1881, he injected six cows, 24 sheep, and a goat with weakened

Cholera is a deadly disease that affects the intestine. It was common across the world until recently. It still occurs in war and disaster zones, where sewage systems have broken down. In 1854 English doctor John Snow found that many cholera victims in London (below) drank water from a single well. He concluded correctly that disease was carried in this water. When the well was closed, the number of new cholera cases fell. The bacteria that cause cholera was not identified until the 1880s.

anthrax bacteria. The bacteria had been weakened by growing them at high temperature. A fortnight later, he injected the animals again, but this time with untreated anthrax bacteria. All 31 animals survived. A similar number of animals that he had injected only once, using just the untreated anthrax, died.

Pasteur's success drove him on to try to find new vaccines for diseases. His next project was rabies, which kills by affecting the nervous system. The French scientist faced problems from the outset and soon found that he was unable to grow the microorganism responsible. Although it was not known at the time, rabies is caused not by a bacterium, but by a virus, a simpler disease-causing agent. Despite this difficulty, Pasteur persevered and eventually managed to make a rabies vaccine using the spinal cords of rabbits

infected with the disease. As part of his preparation, he dried out the spinal cords, which weakened the virus.

Pasteur tried out his rabies vaccine on dogs and found that it worked. But because of the deadly nature of the disease, he was reluctant to test it on people. Then, in 1885, a nine-year-old boy called Joseph Meister, who had been savagely bitten by a rabid dog, was brought to Pasteur. In a final attempt to try to save the boy's life, Pasteur used his vaccine. To everybody's surprise, including Pasteur's, the boy survived. The dog vaccine worked as a cure for humans, too.

THE EFFECT ON HEALTHCARE

The new understanding of how disease was caused led to a huge change in the way people lived their lives and how hospitals were run. Cleanliness and hygiene, which had previously not even been considered by most people, suddenly became all-important. Simple procedures, such as washing hands and instruments before operations, saved lives.

The concept of sanitation was driven home by several medical figures. The English surgeon Joseph Lister (1827–1912) pioneered aseptic surgery, operating in a germ-free environment. He also introduced the concept of sterilizing surgical equipment with chemicals. He used weak carbolic acid to kill bacteria, spraying it on wounds

and bandages as well as scalpels and other tools of his trade. At the time, many other surgeons thought that Lister was eccentric. But as the number of people with infections from his operations dropped, they began to realize that what he was doing worked. In the 1880s, carbolic acid was replaced with steam cleaning, which killed more bacteria. Later, surgeons began wearing sterile rubber gloves to reduce the risk of infection from dirt on their hands.

It was not just surgery that was affected, the way that patients were cared for changed as well. After saving many soldiers' lives by introducing sanitary practices to hospitals in the Crimean War, Florence Nightingale returned to

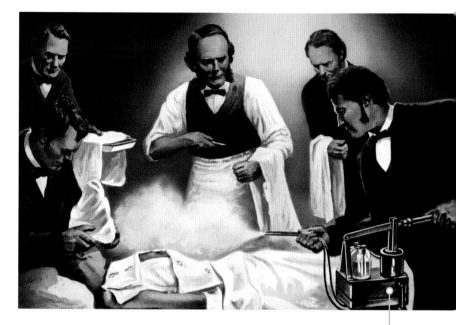

Joseph Lister prepares to operate on a patient. Carbolic acid is sprayed over the patient to stop any cuts from becoming infected.

England determined to educate a new generation of nurses. In 1860, she founded a training college in London. By the end of the 19th century, most nurses were highly trained and had become a crucial

Hypodermic Syringe

Key inventions

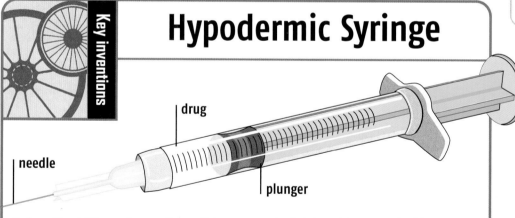

needle

drug

plunger

Before the 19th century, all medicine was administered by mouth. Then, around 1850, French surgeon Charles Gabriel Pravaz (1791–1853) and Scottish doctor Alexander Wood (1817–84) independently began injecting morphine beneath the skin using a syringe, a glass tube and plunger with a hollow metal needle. Pravaz and Wood found that this new method enabled them to control doses more accurately. The drug also acted much faster and could be injected at the site where pain was worse. Before long, news of the invention traveled and use of hypodermic (literally "under skin") syringes became widespread. Today, glass tubes have been replaced with plastic ones. They have a scale marked so drug doses can be measured accurately. Modern syringe needles are disposed of rather than sterilized and reused.

Psychiatry

As the scientific approach became established in Western medicine, some doctors began considering the possibility of applying it to mental disorders and diseases of the mind. Towards the end of the 19th century, the new discipline of psychiatry (literally "mind healing") was born.

Emil Kraepelin (1856–1926) was among the most influential of the early psychiatrists. This German scientist believed that mental illness was caused by physical changes to the brain. Kraepelin's laboratory had recently shown that dementia in old age had a physical origin, and it seemed logical that other sicknesses of the mind must also be caused in this way.

In 1885, the now-famous Austrian biologist Sigmund Freud (1856–1939) came up with a new theory to explain mental problems. He thought that some conditions were caused by the mind unconsciously repressing sexual or aggressive thoughts. In order to treat patients, Freud (above) developed the technique of psychoanalysis to reveal their innermost attitudes and feelings. This involved him discussing many things with them, including their childhoods and dreams. Once Freud had the information he needed, he then tried to cure his patients by explaining what he considered their repressed thoughts and emotions to be. By bringing these to the attention of the conscious mind, he was able to change their personalities in a positive way.

Another important early figure in psychiatry was the Swiss biologist Hermann Rorschach (1884–1922). He developed a psychoanalytical test in which patients were shown a series of ink-blots and asked what images came to mind. The nature of their replies enabled him to explore their fantasies without questioning them. Carl Jung, another Swiss psychoanalyst, obtained similar results by word association. The techniques of Rorschach, Freud, and Jung are still used by psychoanalysts.

NURSES

Florence Nightingale was known as the "Lady with the Lamp" by the soldiers recovering in her military hospital. She would often visit wards at night to see if her patients were alright.

Nurses play a vital role in modern medical practice. While doctors are trained to diagnose illness and prescribe relevant treatments, nurses provide patients with day-to-day care. They do everything from making up beds to administering medicine. Traditionally, most nurses have been women but men work in the profession, too.

Nursing began in families. When a person fell ill, a family member, generally a woman, attended to them. If an ill person was being treated in a hospital, this role was often performed by a monk or nun. Nursing as we know it today began when Florence Nightingale (1820–1910) left Britain to treat soldiers in the Crimean War (1853–56).

Florence Nightingale's father, William, was a wealthy landowner involved in the anti-slavery movement. With no sons of his own, William treated Florence as he would have a boy, educating her in mathematics, history, philosophy, and languages.

At the age of 25, Nightingale announced she wanted to be a nurse. Florence's mother was appalled, since she saw nursing as beneath her. Nevertheless, Florence followed her dream. A meeting with Elizabeth Blackwell (1821–1910) at London's St. Bartholomew's Hospital reinforced her resolve. Blackwell was the first woman doctor in the United States.

In 1851, William Nightingale gave his daughter permission to train as a nurse, and she

Lillian Wald was a nursing pioneer in the United States. She provided basic healthcare to immigrants in 19th-century New York City.

left for Kaiserwerth, Germany, to study at the Institute of Protestant Deaconesses. Two years later, aged 33, she returned to Britain and became Lady Superintendent at a London hospital for disabled women.

When the Crimean War broke out in 1853 with Britain, Turkey, and France fighting Russia, Nightingale volunteered her services. Eventually, she was given permission to take a team of nurses to the war zone. The terrible conditions she found there shocked her. Wounded soldiers were kept in filthy rooms without blankets or proper food. Many were still

in uniforms "stiff with dirt and gore." The sick soldiers shared beds, and most of them died from diseases, such as typhoid or cholera, not from their wounds. Within months, Nightingale had made the hospital a much healthier institution. She told British newspapers about the terrible conditions the wounded were kept in. After the battle at Inkerman, the army were forced to grant Nightingale permission to reorganize the hospital. The improvement in sanitation she made greatly reduced the number of deaths from disease, and when Florence returned to Britain she was a national heroine.

Many other 19th and 20th century nurses followed Florence Nightingale's example to reform and expand the profession. In the United States, there are two women who perhaps did more than anyone else. In 1895, Lillian Wald (1867–1940) founded the Henry Street Settlement in New York's Lower East Side. The Settlement was set up to cater to poor immigrant families and was among the first of its kind in the country. Although from a privileged background, Wald chose to live among the people she worked with. It was she who introduced the pioneering concept of "public

health nursing," bringing medical care within reach of those too poor to otherwise afford it.

Mary Breckinridge (1881–1965) did for poor rural communities what Wald had begun in the cities. After the deaths of her husband and two children, she devoted her life to caring for the disadvantaged. In 1925, Breckinridge founded the Frontier Nursing Service. She also introduced nurse-midwifery services to poor people in the countryside.

Early nurses followed strict discipline. Their uniforms were kept very clean to prevent passing on infections.

25

MAKING A DIAGNOSIS

The electrical activity of a human heart is displayed on a computer. Doctors can see problems in the way the heart is working by studying these graphs.

Identifying what is wrong with a patient is diagnosis. Diagnostic techniques have improved many times over in the past 300 years. Doctors once had to rely on what patients could tell them about their symptoms to figure out what the problem was. Now they have tools that can pick up a variety of tell-tale signs. For example, blood pressure can be measured and samples of body fluids analysed. There are even machines that can look inside patients without them feeling a thing.

MEDICAL INSTRUMENTS

One of the first modern aids to diagnosis was the stethoscope, invented in the early 19th century. The stethoscope allows doctors to listen to sounds inside the body, such as the heartbeat.

It was followed by the ophthalmoscope, devised by the German physicist Hermann von Helmholtz in 1851. This device enabled doctors to examine the interior of the eye, in particular, the retina, which has the only visible blood vessels in the body.

Key inventions

Stethoscope

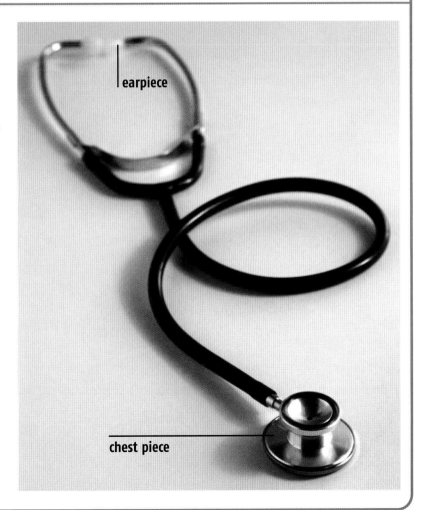

earpiece

chest piece

The invention of the stethoscope in 1815 marked the beginning of a new chapter in diagnostic medicine. For the first time, doctors could hear clearly what was going on inside the heart, lungs, and stomach. This new tool added to the list of symptoms, enabling quicker and more accurate diagnosis of many diseases.

The stethoscope was invented by Frenchman René Laënnec (1781–1826). This early model was somewhat different to those used today. It was a wooden tube with a pointed ear piece at one end and a rounded cup at the other. Just like today's models, it worked by concentrating sounds from the body. Modern stethoscopes have a chest piece holding a sensitive diaphragm and a tube leading to each ear. They have been in use since the end of the 19th century.

Examination

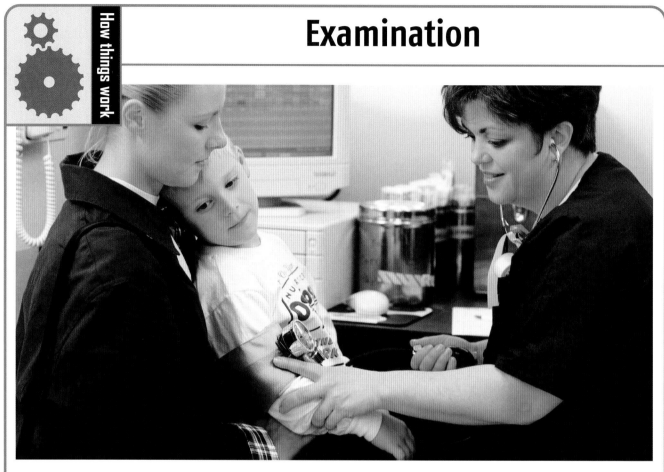

The first point of contact for most people with the medical world is the health center or doctor's office. Here mild and life-threatening illnesses are diagnosed every day. Depending on what they find, doctors working in these places can advise rest, prescribe medicines, or refer patients to see specialist doctors.

Diagnoses are made on the basis of an examination. This usually begins with a series of questions to establish the patient's medical history. Following that, there is the physical examination, during which a doctor may use a number of tools. Temperature might be taken with a medical thermometer and heart rate established using a stopwatch to measure the pulse. A patient's reflexes might be tested by hitting below the knee with a rubber hammer. Blood pressure is measured using a sphygmomanometer (above).

Depending on the nature of the problem, more specialized equipment might be used. Most doctors will have an ophthalmoscope for examining the eyes and an otoscope for looking into the ears. Then, of course, there is the most familiar part of a doctor's equipment, the stethoscope, for examining heartbeat and breathing.

After the physical examination, doctors use their knowledge and experience to diagnose the problem and prescribe a cure. If they are uncertain, they may ask the patient to give a blood or urine sample for analysis and return at a later date.

The ophthalmoscope is now a regular part of most doctor's equipment and retinal examinations are routine. By looking closely at the retina, doctors can catch problems that might affect vision.

Perhaps surprisingly, the thermometer did not appear in the doctor's tool kit until after the ophthalmoscope. The thermometer was invented in 1592 by the Italian physicist Galileo Galilei

(1564–1642). Early versions were too cumbersome for medical use. In 1867, British doctor Thomas Allbutt developed a small clinical thermometer. His device held liquid mercury in a fine glass tube. Modern thermometers are similar but use colored alcohol instead of mercury.

NEW VIEWS

The next major development in diagnosis was the ability to look inside patients using X rays. X rays were discovered by accident in 1895. While experimenting with cathode ray tubes, German physicist Wilhelm Röntgen (1845–1923) noticed that when he turned the tube on, a piece of barium that was near to it

Many medical thermometers used today do not use liquids. Instead they measure body temperature with thermistors. These are semiconductors that produce electricity when they warm up. The temperature is displayed on a digital readout.

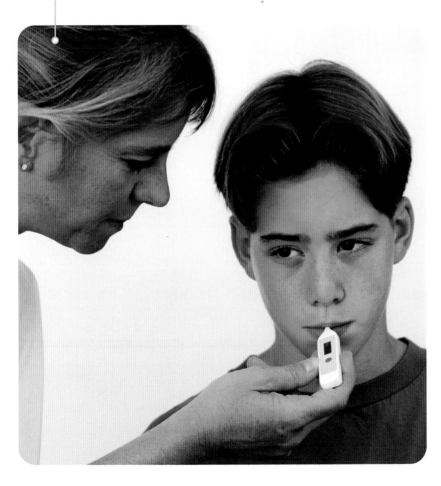

glowed. Although Röntgen could see no light traveling from the tube to the barium, he realized that something must be connecting the two. That something was invisible high-energy waves, which Röntgen called X rays. Later, he found that this new form of radiation could travel through solid materials and create an image on a photographic plate. X rays began to be used to take pictures of people's insides.

As the 20th century began, developments in electrical engineering led to other medical inventions. In 1903, the Dutch doctor Willem Einthoven (1820–1927) built an electrocardiograph (ECG), which recorded a heart's electrical impulses. ECGs are still used to search for irregularities in the heartbeat. Following the ECG was the electroencephalograph (EEG). Invented in 1924 by the German psychiatrist Hans Berger, this device was able to record electrical activity inside the skull, making it useful for helping to diagnose brain disorders.

In 1960, the technique of thermography was developed. This enabled doctors to see the temperatures of different areas of the surface of the body. By examining healthy people, normal human temperature maps were drawn up. Marks that did not fit these patterns could indicate an abnormality. Inflamed areas have higher temperatures than normal, for example, as do tissues that are growing rapidly, which may be a

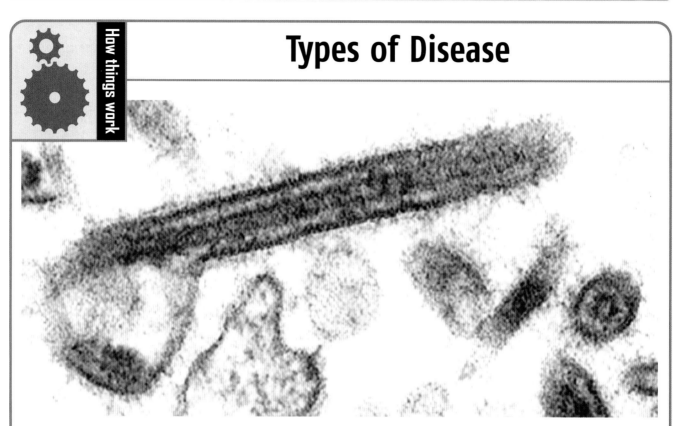

Types of Disease

There are hundreds of different diseases that can affect the human body. Barring physical injury, all of them fall into one of three categories: infectious diseases, hereditary diseases, and diseases caused by exposure to non-living substances in the environment, such as pollution or alcohol.

Infectious diseases are caused by other organisms invading the body and multiplying inside it. Bacteria, viruses, protists (large single-celled organisms, such as amoebas), and fungi can all cause infectious disease. Bacteria produce tuberculosis, anthrax, and cholera, among many other illnesses. They can be killed off, and symptoms cleared, with chemicals called antibiotics.

Viruses are much harder to get rid of. Consisting of nothing more than genetic material surrounded by a protein coat, they depend completely on the cells of other living organisms to reproduce and survive. They cannot be destroyed by antibiotics. Vaccines exist for some viral diseases, such as smallpox, but many other viruses, such as those that cause common colds or ebola (above), cannot be tackled directly by medicines.

Protists are complex, single-celled organisms. Unlike bacteria, they have cells that are just as complex as those of animals and plants. Most

protists are harmless, but a few cause terrible diseases, such as sleeping sickness and malaria. Most protists can be combated with drugs.

Fungi may be single-celled and multicellular organisms that feed on living or dead organic matter. The diseases they cause are rarely fatal. One of the most common is athlete's foot. Fungal infections can be treated with antifungal powders or other drugs.

Hereditary diseases are caused by problem genes that are passed down through families. They include cystic fibrosis and sickle-cell anaemia. While they cannot currently be cured, they can be treated to tackle symptoms and improve a sufferer's quality of life.

Diseases caused by external factors include liver, lung, and heart problems produced by smoking, drinking alcohol, and eating a poor diet. Cancers may be caused by external factors. Substances that cause cancer, such as cigarette smoke, are called carcinogens.

 Fact Doctors divide diseases into two types. A disease that develops quickly but also goes away again is described as acute. A chronic disease is one that persists for a very long time.

signal of cancer. Thermography was just one of a range of new techniques for looking into the body without having to cut it open. Others include computerized axial tomography (CAT) scanning, magnetic resonance imaging (MRI) and positron emission tomography (PET) scanning.

TAKING SAMPLES

Diagnosis may be made by direct observation or looking at scans. A third approach is to take samples for analysis. There are five main types of sample a doctor might collect: blood, urine, feces, cells, and tissue. Examining urine and feces for symptoms of disease is a practice that dates back centuries. Analysing the other three types of sample has only become common in recent years with the invention of advanced testing equipment.

Blood and urine are generally tested by running them through a machine called a biochemical analyzer. This can measure the quantities of a wide range of substances in the liquids. To prepare blood for testing, it is spun at high speed to separate out the cells from the liquid plasma. It is the plasma that is tested by a biochemical analyzer.

To search for a particular substance in a sample, a chemical is added which changes color when it comes into contact with that substance. The machine shines a light beam through the sample to measure the intensity of the color. It then uses that information to calculate the quantity of the substance present.

Cell and tissue samples are usually taken to diagnose genetic disorders and cancers. Cells may be removed painlessly using a plastic stick with a cotton end, known as a swab. Tissue samples are cut out with a scalpel (sharp surgical knife) or sucked out through a biopsy needle. This looks like a large hypodermic syringe. Cell and tissue samples are examined by putting them under a microscope to look for abnormal cells.

Doctors that study the causes of diseases are called pathologists. Here a pathologist is slicing into a sample of tumor that has been cut from a person's brain. The cells in the sample, or biopsy, will be tested to see if the tumor is cancerous.

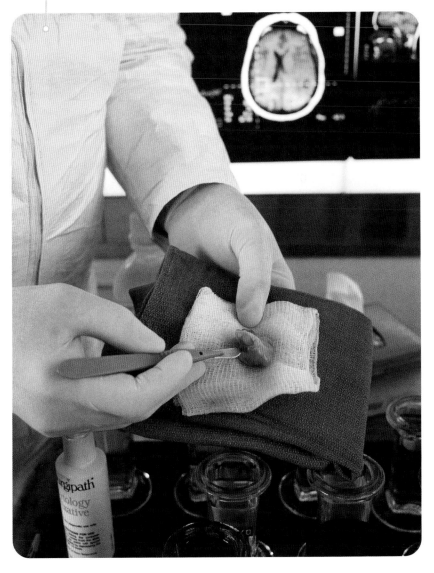

LOOKING INSIDE

X-Ray Machine

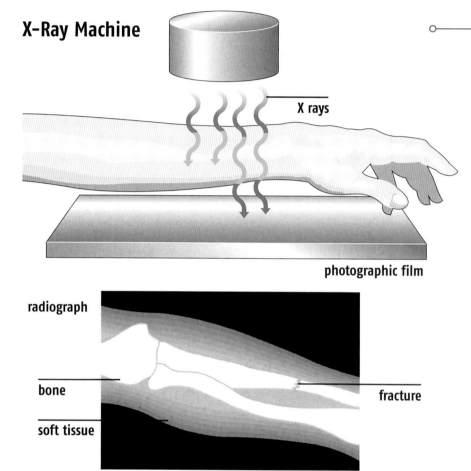

X rays

photographic film

radiograph

bone

soft tissue

fracture

High-energy X rays pass right through soft tissues, but they do not get through solid bones and other hard tissue. The X rays that get through hit a photographic film making it darken. The shadow of bones appears as white areas on the film.

In the past, if doctors wanted to find the exact cause of an internal problem, they often had no choice but to cut a patient open. Today, there are a range of machines that let doctors look inside without surgery.

Some produce pictures and are known as non-invasive imaging devices. Others, called endoscopes, can enter through natural body openings, or orifices, to give an internal view.

The most familiar non-invasive imaging device is the X-ray machine. X rays were discovered in 1895 by Wilhelm Röntgen. He produced images, or radiographs, of his hand, which showed the bones inside. The first medical use of X rays was in the Balkan War of 1897, when they were used to locate bullets inside patients before surgery. Today they are used to examine bone fractures and other solid tissue problems, such as arthritis.

While radiographs are useful, they have their limits. Soft tissue, such as an organ, is not shown clearly. So cancerous growths, for example, are often hard to spot. In 1950, ultrasound techniques were developed. These bounce high-frequency sound waves off tissues. The echoes are turned into images that show soft tissue more clearly. Ultrasound imaging is most used to show parents images of their unborn babies.

Computerized axial tomography (CAT) scanning gives more precise views of growths in the body. CAT scanning was developed in 1972 and uses a computer to produce 3-D images of organs. These are built up from many cross-sections taken with X rays. As well as tumors and other soft tissue, it shows cavities inside the body, such as the stomach and lungs.

Ultrasound Imaging

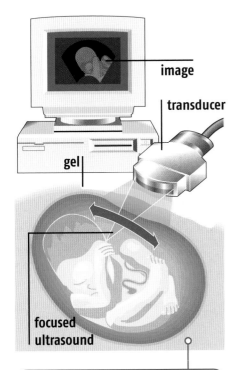

image

transducer

gel

focused ultrasound

A gel focuses the sound waves into the body. Echoes from inside the body are detected by the transducer. They are interpreted by a computer, which displays them as a moving image.

Like CAT scanning, magnetic resonance imaging (MRI) shows soft tissue and body cavities, as well as hard structures, such as teeth. It works by using a device that surrounds the body with a

MRI scanners use a magnet to line up atoms inside the body. Radio waves are used to knock the atoms briefly out of alignment. As they line up again, the atoms release a tiny radio signal. These signals are used to build a detailed image.

strong magnetic field. The field is then scanned with radio waves. MRI images are extremely detailed and have been used by doctors since the technology was first introduced in 1980.

Another non-invasive technique is positron emission tomography (PET) scanning. Small amounts of radioactive material are injected into a patient's body. They reveal how cells are functioning. PET scanning is often used to show brain activity and is widely used in research.

Over the years, several variations of non-invasive imaging have been developed. Contrast radiographs, for example, are used to show

hollow structures, such as intestine. They use barium liquid, which shows up on X-ray radiographs, when it is swallowed or injected.

Endoscopes are imaging devices that enter the body. They have been used by doctors for more than a century. The earliest devices were short, rigid tubes used to look inside the bladder or colon. Today, flexible endoscopes are used. They have optical fibers, which can transmit color video images from inside a patient. Flexible endoscopes can enter any opening, including the mouth. They are used to look for blockages or damage to internal tissues.

MRI Scans

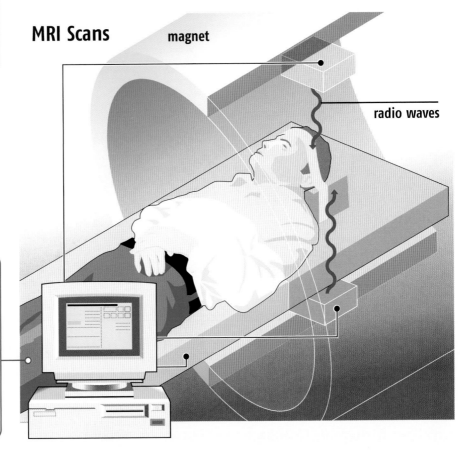

magnet

radio waves

TAKING MEDICINE

Medical drugs are substances taken to treat or cure disease. People have used them for thousands of years. As long ago as 3000 B.C.E., people in China were making medicines from plant parts and animal extracts. Later, the Egyptians also recorded that some plants had healing qualities. Plant sap and tree resins (sticking liquids found in bark) were used to treat skin conditions. A wide variety of preparations were taken for internal complaints. Many of these ancient medicines worked and some are still used today.

Castor oil, for example, was taken to lubricate the digestive system 3,000 years ago, just as it is now.

OPIATES AND ASPIRIN

Today, medicine is more of an exact science, and drugs are prepared in sterile conditions to precise specifications. Nevertheless, many of their ingredients are still either derived from plants or made to closely match plant chemicals. The most powerful painkillers, for example, are based on chemicals called opiates. These are produced in the seed-heads of poppies. In

Many children are given drugs called vaccines. These medicines protect the children from diseases. People who are traveling abroad to places where diseases are a problem may also be vaccinated.

south and eastern Asia poppies grow wild. There, the effects of opium, the raw poppy extract, have been known for centuries. When smoked, opium is a highly addictive drug, but one of its effects is that it dulls pain. Opium was long used in China and other Asian countries as a source of pain relief. In the 19th century, three new drugs, morphine, codeine, and thebaine, were isolated from opium by scientists. Morphine was discovered by German Friedrich Wilhelm Sertürner (1783–1841) in 1803. This drug remains the most potent painkiller in general use by doctors. However, morphine is not available in drug stores because, like opium, it is highly addictive. Codeine, on the other hand, is available over the counter, at least on prescription. Today, both morphine and codeine can be made chemically without having to uses natural opium.

Key inventions

Painkillers

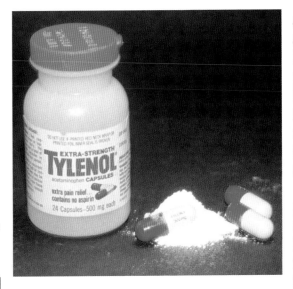

Painkillers are widely used in modern medicine. Many are available in drugstores for use at home. Painkillers fall into two main categories—narcotic and non-narcotic.

Narcotic painkillers are much more powerful and can be used to relieve any level of pain. They block pain signals carried along nerves in the spinal cord and brain. Nerve receptors that would normally receive the chemicals that transmit pain are filled up by the narcotic drug instead. The main narcotics are morphine, codeine, and tramadol.

Non-narcotic painkillers are used to treat mild to moderate pain. These drugs work by slowing the body's production of prostaglandins. These are chemicals that make areas of tissue swell up and become more sensitive to pain. Unlike narcotic painkillers, non-narcotics work at the site of the injury itself. As prostaglandin production slows, so does the discomfort. The one exception to this rule is acetaminophen (above right). Although classed as a non-narcotic, acetaminophen works like a narcotic, blocking pain impulses in the brain. Unlike other non-narcotics, it does not reduce swelling, but it will reduce a high temperature.

Because many painkillers work by different mechanisms, it is possible to combine them to provide relief for varied levels of pain. Unless pain is truly severe, narcotic drugs may be tempered by mixing them with non-narcotics. Similarly, non-narcotic painkillers can be boosted by adding small doses of narcotics to them. These combination painkillers are often available over the counter, as remedies for headaches, backache, and other minor disorders. Common combinations include codeine with aspirin or acetaminophen. Most narcotic drugs, however, can only be administered by doctors. Many have side effects, such as nausea or drowsiness. They will kill if the dose is too high.

Aspirin is another painkiller with a long history. Willow bark has been used as a medicine for a long time. Strips of the bark were chewed to relieve everything from labor pains to headaches. In 1897, German chemist Felix Hoffman (1868–1946) linked the bark's effects with the salicylic acid it contained. He used the bark to make acetylsalicylic acid, and sold this as a painkiller. In 1899, this drug was renamed as aspirin.

Aspirin was initially a painkiller, but today is also used to treat people at risk of strokes. Strokes are caused by blood clots lodging in vessels in the brain. Aspirin thins the blood and prevents clots from forming.

A CENTURY OF DISCOVERY

Most of the drugs used today were discovered in the past 100 years. In 1910, German chemist Paul Ehrlich (1854–1915) developed salvarsan to treat syphilis, a deadly disease spread during sexual contact. Salvarsan was the first completely artificial drug designed to tackle a specific disease. Salvarsan was followed by penicillin, the world's first antibiotic. Identified by Alexander Fleming (1881–1955) in 1928, it went on to revolutionize the way infectious diseases were treated. Penicillin was developed commercially in 1940, by two men, German Ernst Chain (1906–79) and an Australian named Howard Florey (1898–1968). They were awarded for this work with the Nobel Prize for Medicine. They shared the honor with Fleming.

At first aspirin was sold as powder and liquid. It did not appear as tablets until 1915. The German drug company Bayer was the first to sell aspirin. After World War I (1914–18), however, the company was forced to allow foreign companies to make it, too.

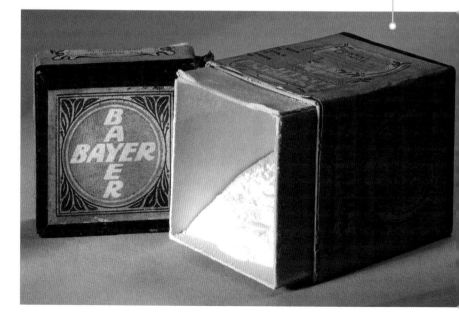

Fighting Malaria

How things work

Malaria is one of the world's most deadly diseases. Although confined to warm, tropical areas, it is estimated to kill at least two million people every year.

Malaria is caused by single-celled organisms called *Plasmodium*, which infect a person's bloodstream and liver. Once they are in the body, it is almost impossible to get rid of these invaders since they hide inside the red blood cells or liver cells themselves. Fortunately, there are no symptoms until the protist emerges into the blood stream. This happens as the parasite reproduces, breaking out of the red blood cells. The infected person then suffers from fever, muscle pain, and if he or she is not treated, will eventually die.

People are infected with malaria when they are bitten by a female *Anopholes* mosquito. These insects feed on blood and carry *Plasmodium* in the saliva. Mosquitoes can be kept away with nets and repellent, but anyone who lives in a malarial area will be bitten at some point.

Although there is no vaccine for malaria, there are several drugs that help prevent infections. If these fail to work, and the disease develops, stronger drugs are used to kill off the *Plasmodium*. Most of these medicines are based on the natural substance quinine. The antimalarial properties of quinine have been known for hundreds of years. The bark of the cinchona tree, which contains quinine, has been chewed by South American people to relieve malarial fever since long before Christopher Columbus reached America.

Today, most antimalarial drugs are synthetic forms of quinine, produced in a factory. Some, such as chloroquine, are taken as tablets to

1. A female mosquito sucks in blood from a person infected with malaria. The *Plasmodium* are also sucked into the insect's stomach.

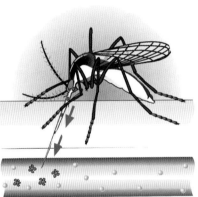

salivary gland

stomach

Plasmodium

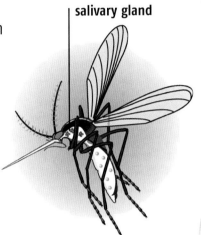

2. The *Plasmodium* travel to the insect's salivary glands.

3. When the insect bites another person, the *Plasmodium* are injected in the blood.

prevent the bugs from getting a hold in the first place. Mefloquine and primaquine are used to combat outbreaks of fever in people who are already infected. Unfortunately, the *Plasmodium* protists that cause malaria keep evolving resistance to the synthetic drugs, meaning that stronger forms are always being developed. Quinine still defeats all types of malarial parasites, but doctors must use this very sparingly to prevent resistance developing to that drug too.

★ Fact In the 1950s, chemicals were used to kill mosquitoes and reduce the size of malarial areas. Now spraying has stopped, mosquitoes are returning to many cleared areas.

Perhaps the two other greatest achievements in medicine in the 20th century were the discovery of streptomycin in 1943, and the vaccine for polio in 1954. Streptomycin was an incredible find in that it was a cure for both tuberculosis and meningitis. The drug was discovered by a young American postgraduate student named Albert Schatz.

The first vaccine for polio was created by the American Jonas Salk (1914–95). In 1961, another American, Albert Sabin (1906–93), developed a new form of this drug that could be swallowed.

DRUG DEVELOPMENT TODAY

Drug companies spend huge sums of money developing new drugs. A useful drug would be taken by millions of people and make the company a lot of money.

Modern medicines are developed with the help of computers. They model how a drug and body chemicals will interact with each other, and scientists can visualize the shape of the drug they have to create. Before any drug is actually used on a patient, it is rigorously tested on living tissue, generally of other animals, to make sure that it is safe.

A pharmacologist (drug scientist) uses 3-D glasses to study a computer model of Prozac. This drug is used to control depression.

When Drugs Go Wrong

Medical drugs have saved the lives of millions of people, and improved the quality of life for millions more. But unfortunately they have caused some people problems that they did not have before. Most drugs have side effects, and some people become addicted to them. In the late 1970s, as many as 10 million Americans were estimated to be addicted to the tranquilizer Valium, a prescription drug used to relieve stress.

Side effects are undesired reactions that result from a normal dose of the drug. For example, some drugs cause drowsiness or nausea. Some side effects, such as drug allergies, can be more serious. In rare cases, a drug's side effects may not become apparent until long after it is taken. In the 1950s, many pregnant women used a sleeping pill known as thalidomide. This drug was found to deform the limbs of their unborn children (above).

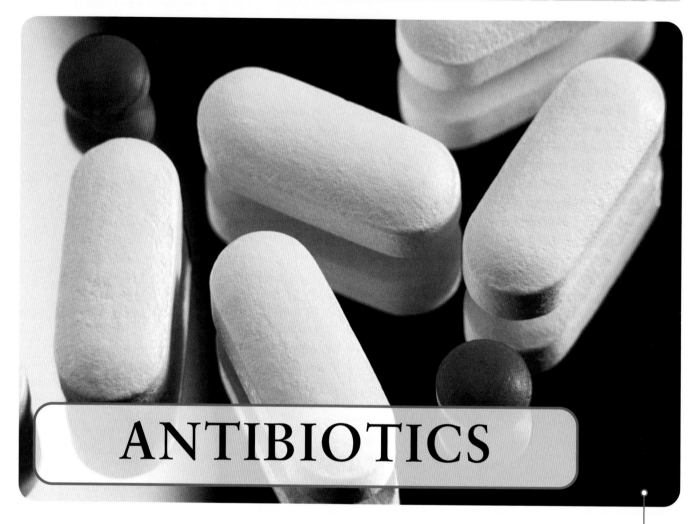

ANTIBIOTICS

Drugs in one form or another have been with us for thousands of years, but antibiotics are a relatively recent development. The first antibiotic, penicillin, was isolated in 1928. Like many of the greatest breakthroughs in science and medicine, its discovery was an accident.

The effects of penicillin were first noticed in 1871 by a Scottish surgeon Joseph Lister (1827–1912). During research on germs in the air, Lister observed that when certain molds were present, the bacteria he was studying failed to grow properly. Lister realized that something in the molds was killing the bacteria and conducted experiments to try to find out what it was. He failed to identify what was responsible and turned his attention to other work.

Almost 60 years later, another Scot rediscovered what Lister had seen. In 1928, while studying the bacteria that make wounds go septic, Alexander Fleming (1881–1955) found mold near one of his specimen dishes. When he looked at the dish, Fleming saw that there were far less bacteria growing on it than usual. He, too, reasoned

Antibiotics are available as pills or capsules. Children are given antibiotics in liquid medicines, while the very sick have the drugs pumped straight into their blood.

that the mold was preventing the bacteria from growing. Later that year, Fleming managed to isolate a crude extract of the mold's active agent, which he named penicillin. Fleming tested his discovery and found that it was effective against the bacteria that caused many diseases, including anthrax, diptheria, and meningitis. He

Alexander Fleming in his laboratory. He came across penicillin, the first antibiotic, by accident.

published these findings but had to stop his research because of a lack of funds.

It was not until World War II (1939–45) that research into the effects of penicillin was able to begin again. In 1939, at England's Oxford University, Australian Howard Florey (1898–1968) teamed up with Ernst Chain (1906–79), a German Jew who had fled the Nazis. Building on Fleming's work, the two scientists developed the drug. In 1945, they and Fleming were jointly awarded the Nobel Prize for Medicine.

Today, penicillin is just one of several antibiotics used to treat all manner of infections and diseases. Other, less well-known, examples include erythromycin, sulfadiazine, and tetracycline. Some antibiotics tackle a wide range of illnesses, but many others are used to target specific problems. Antibiotics

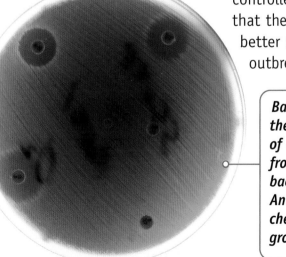

Bacteria are grown in the laboratory on a dish of agar. This gel is made from seaweed. The bacteria feed on it. Antibiotics are tested by checking which bacteria grow in their presence.

exist that can kill protists as well as bacteria. Most are swallowed by patients although they may also be injected or used in eye drops.

Antibiotics work in one of two ways. Some actually destroy the bacteria they target. Penicillin, for example, does this by breaking down the bacteria's protective cell walls. Other antibiotics alter chemical processes within bacteria to prevent them from reproducing. The remaining bacteria are then killed off by the body's immune system.

Antibiotics are prescribed in huge amounts all over the world. They are also often given to farm animals to prevent disease and maximize growth. Unfortunately, several microorganisms are evolving resistance to antibiotics, becoming dangerous "superbugs." Many doctors suggest that antibiotics should be used less to prevent this from happening again. More controlled use would mean that these drugs could be better relied on to treat outbreaks of serious illness.

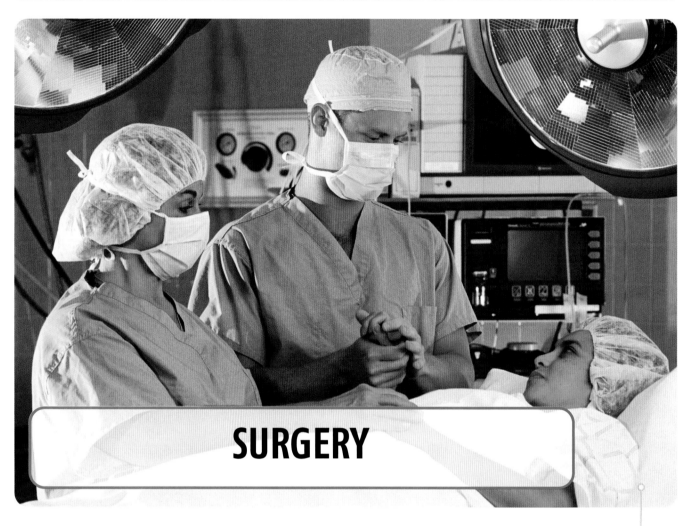

SURGERY

Surgery is the most extreme form of medicine, cutting the body open in order to remove the cause of disease or repair injuries. For thousands of years, surgery was conducted without anesthetic. Unless they fainted, patients remained awake throughout the entire procedure. Most operations were amputations. Surgeons could not cut into the abdomen because the shock and pain would kill the patient. Today, operations are performed without patients feeling a thing. In many cases, they may be kept unconscious for several hours, and doctors operate on just about all areas of the body.

ANCIENT OPERATIONS
People have been practicing surgery since before history began. Evidence suggests that trepanning was common among prehistoric cultures. It seems likely that other types of operations were performed too.

The earliest historical records we have of surgery taking place come from Mesopotamia (modern Iraq) and ancient Egypt. Most operations were minor ones, such as repositioning dislocated bones or sewing up flesh wounds. Most other ailments were treated with herbal remedies and spells. Because it was so dangerous and painful, surgery was very much a

Although modern surgery is always a major procedure, drugs and technology make it safer than ever before. Patients generally meet their surgeons before the operation begins, when the surgeons explain what they will do.

last resort. In cases that demanded it, however, such as cutting out cysts or tumors, it was carried out.

Surgical methods were recorded by the ancient Egyptians on scrolls made from a plant called papyrus. The first surgical textbook did not appear until the 4th century B.C.E., however. It was written in India by a surgeon called Sushruta and is known as the *Sushruta-samhita*. The *Sushruta-samhita* details complex surgical procedures and describes operations to remove

Surgical Equipment

How things work

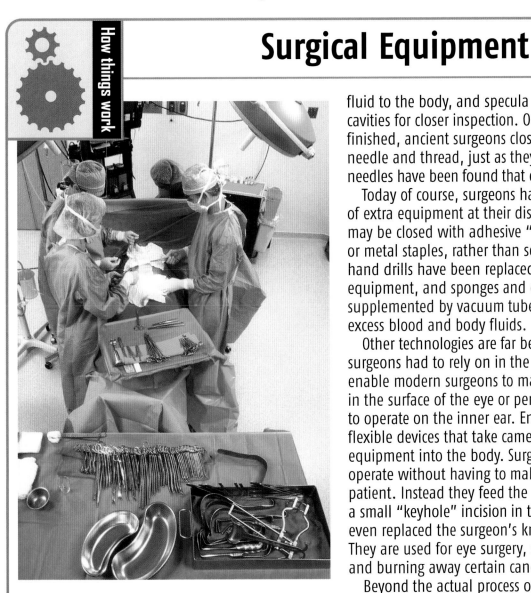

Some parts of the surgeon's tool kit have not changed in millennia. Hieroglyphs from ancient Egypt show that many pieces of equipment familiar to surgeons today were already in use then, more than 4,000 years ago. The scalpel was already well developed, and surgeons had sponges, drills, forceps, and various probes. There were even catheters for introducing or removing

fluid to the body, and specula to pull open body cavities for closer inspection. Once operations were finished, ancient surgeons closed wounds with a needle and thread, just as they do today. Surgical needles have been found that date from 3000 B.C.E.

Today of course, surgeons have a whole range of extra equipment at their disposal (left). Wounds may be closed with adhesive "butterfly" stitches or metal staples, rather than sewn. Handsaws and hand drills have been replaced with mechanized equipment, and sponges and catheters are now supplemented by vacuum tubes for sucking out excess blood and body fluids.

Other technologies are far beyond what early surgeons had to rely on in the past. Microscopes enable modern surgeons to make precise incisions in the surface of the eye or penetrate the eardrum to operate on the inner ear. Endoscopes are flexible devices that take cameras and surgical equipment into the body. Surgeons use them to operate without having to make large cuts in the patient. Instead they feed the endoscope through a small "keyhole" incision in the skin. Lasers have even replaced the surgeon's knife in some cases. They are used for eye surgery, skin treatments, and burning away certain cancers.

Beyond the actual process of surgery itself, patient safety has been greatly improved during operations. The patient's vital signs, such as blood pressure, heart rate, and oxygen levels, are constantly monitored by an electrocardiograph (ECG). The patient is kept unconscious by anesthetic gases fed directly into the lungs. This tube also keeps them supplied with the right amount of oxygen.

kidney stones, treat battle wounds, and even remodel facial features. Sushruta is widely regarded as the father of plastic surgery. His book contains the first records of rhinoplasty—reconstructive surgery of the nose. In India at the time, having one's nose cut off was the punishment for adultery, and it seems that surgeons had plenty of cases to perfect their skills.

BLOOD AND PAIN

After Sushruta's time, the skill of surgeons in India gradually declined. The rest of the world was not to see anything like it for hundreds of years. In fact, there were no significant advances in surgery until the mid-19th century. It was at that point that the first anesthetics appeared. These were drugs that numbed patients to the agony of surgery.

Even after the appearance of anesthetics, surgeons were not willing to operate unless there was absolutely no other option. The reason for this was the danger of a patient dying, either from blood loss or infection.

The problem of surgical wounds becoming infected was reduced after surgeons began working in aseptic (germ-free) conditions. Later, antibiotics helped patients fight off infections while they recovered from the surgery.

Blood loss during surgery was a more complex problem because it depended on which body part was being cut into. Many people died

Heart and Lung Machine

This machine takes over the job of a patient's heart and lungs during an operation. Before it was invented in 1952, surgeons could not operate inside the heart without killing the patient.

1. Blood lacking oxygen is pumped from the heart and main veins into the machine.

2. Bubbles in the blood are removed in a defoamer.

3. Oxygen is added to the blood. A stirrer helps to maximize the oxygen in the blood.

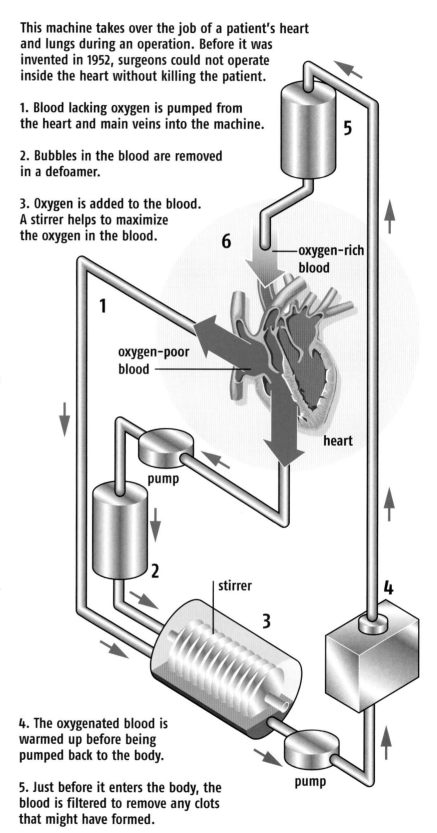

oxygen-rich blood

oxygen-poor blood

heart

pump

stirrer

pump

4. The oxygenated blood is warmed up before being pumped back to the body.

5. Just before it enters the body, the blood is filtered to remove any clots that might have formed.

6. The blood is pumped into the main arteries and on around the body.

Implants

Surgery is about more than just treating injuries or removing dangerous tumors. Organs can be transplanted into the body from other people or synthetic objects inserted for medical purposes. Synthetic objects inserted surgically are known as implants. They include artificial organs, joints, and other body parts, as well as slow-release drug supplies, and devices such as pacemakers, which regulate heartbeat.

Most implant surgery is conducted for reasons of health. People suffering from the pain of arthritis can have joints made of plastic, ceramic, or metal to replace worn-down ends of bones. The most commonly replaced joint is the hip, with more than 800,000 operations performed around the world every year. Pacemakers, vital to prevent heart attacks, are also fitted in huge numbers. Current estimates put the global annual total at around 300,000.

Cosmetic surgery in now very popular. Silicon breast implants and nose reshaping are the most common. While they serve no medical need, these procedures can be important in raising a person's self-esteem. Other cosmetic implant procedures include lip enhancement, where synthetic tissue is added to plump up lips.

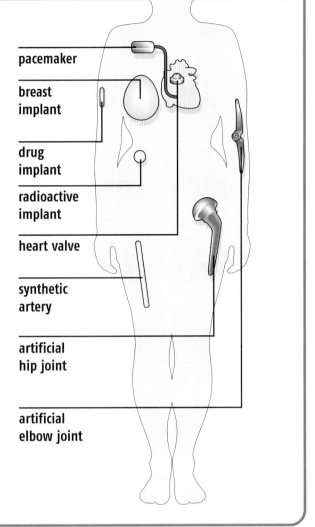

pacemaker

breast implant

drug implant

radioactive implant

heart valve

synthetic artery

artificial hip joint

artificial elbow joint

from it well into the 20th century before technology was developed to help the patient's blood supply. Since William Harvey (1578–1657) figured out how the blood system worked in 1628, surgeons began replacing blood being lost in operations with blood transfusions. But many early transfusions killed the patients, who experienced terrible reactions to the new blood. In 1900, the Austrian-born U.S. scientist Karl Landsteiner (1868–1943) discovered blood groups. Landsteiner identified two proteins on the surfaces of blood cells, antigen A and antigen B. He found that people's blood fell into one of four groups, A, B, AB, and O. Group A blood (with just antigen A) was destroyed by the immune system if is was given to someone who had group B blood (with just antigen B). AB blood contained both antigens, while the O group contained neither. Doctors now match blood to their patients before beginning transfusions.

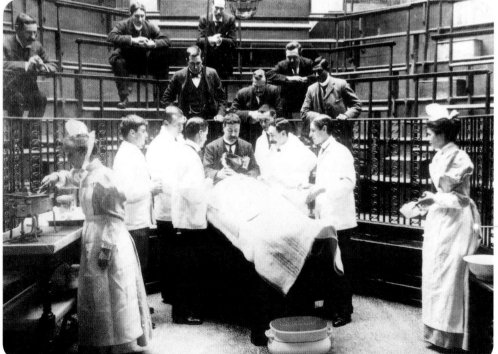

Until around 150 years ago, most surgeons were not doctors, but barbers. As well as cutting hair, they carried out basic surgical procedures.

19th-century surgeons often operated in front of an audience. Modern operating rooms are still sometimes known as theaters.

Anesthetics

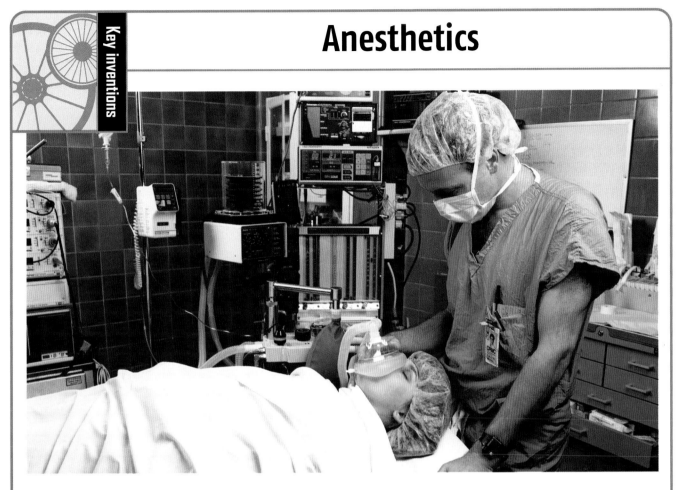

Although it is hard to imagine, less than 250 years ago all operations were undertaken without any anesthetic. Patients were sometimes given alcoholic drinks to try to dull the pain but this rarely had much impact. As one surviving amputee put it, awaiting an operation was like being "a condemned criminal preparing for an execution." Fortunately for everyone alive today who has had or will have surgery, anesthetic is now routinely used around the world.

The first anesthetic was nitrous oxide, or laughing gas, discovered by the English chemist Humphry Davy (1778-1829) in 1799. Davy used nitrous oxide on himself, both for pleasure and, later, to stop the pain of having his teeth pulled out. Laughing gas is still used on dental patients and women in labor today.

Nitrous oxide was followed in 1831 by the discovery of chloroform. Chloroform was first used as an anesthetic in 1847 by James Young Simpson (1811–70), the Scottish Professor of Midwifery at Edinburgh University. He gave the liquid to a woman in labor, and she reported giving birth without any pain. The chloroform inhaler, invented in 1885, allowed doses to be more carefully controlled, making use of the substance much safer.

Today, anesthesiology is a medical science in its own right. Anesthesiologists (above) are highly trained doctors responsible solely for administering anesthetic drugs. What they give a patient may calm them before a simple operation, render them completely unconscious, or numb one area of the body. The range of drugs and techniques they use is wide and their understanding of doses precise.

Modern anesthetic drugs are divided into two groups: Those that render the patient unconscious, known as general anesthetics, and those that numb the area to be operated on, known as local anesthetics. Local anesthetics are injected for minor operations, such as removing a mole or stitching a cut. They include benzocaine, lidocaine, and tetracaine. General anesthetics may either be injected or given as gas.

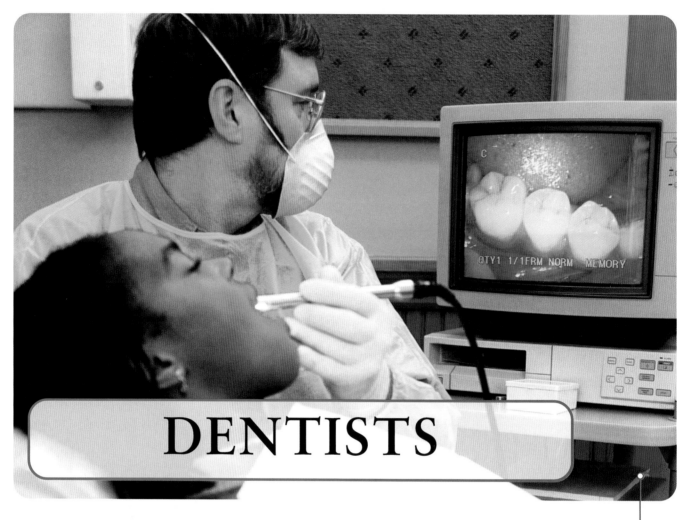

DENTISTS

Modern dentistry is a high-tech business. Tiny cameras give dentists a close-up view of a person's teeth, while X-ray images show what is going on inside the gums.

Like much in the history of medicine, the origins of dentistry date back to the ancient Egyptians. A lower jaw from Egypt thought to be 5,000 years old has two holes drilled through the bone, probably to drain an abscessed tooth. A papyrus scroll dating back even earlier refers to diseases of the teeth and medicines to be applied to the mouth to relieve pain.

It was a Greek called Aesculapius who came up with the idea of removing decayed teeth to prevent toothache in 1300 B.C.E. By 300 B.C.E., Hippocrates and Aristotle had recorded how wires were used to bind loose teeth and reset broken jaws. Two centuries later, the Roman Celsus wrote extensively on gum disease. It seems that dentistry was well understood in ancient Rome, and a variety of treatments were available, including narcotics to soothe and cure bleeding gums.

With the fall of the Roman Empire, dentistry in Europe went into decline, along with most organized medicine. The practice no longer remained specialized, and teeth were pulled by so-called "barber surgeons." These were men who cut hair, stitched wounds, and pulled teeth. The red and white striped barber's pole, still used today represents blood and bandages.

Things finally began to change in the late 17th century. In 1685, the first English book on dentistry, Charles Allen's *The Operator for Teeth*, was published.

48

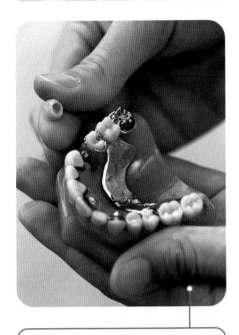

Modern dentures are made from plastic. They are specially molded to fit a person's mouth exactly.

Then, in 1728, Pierre Fauchard (1678–1761) published *The Surgeon Dentist*, a landmark book, which for the first time described dentistry as a modern profession.

Today, dentists are able to fix teeth rather than just remove them. Medieval physicians tried filling tooth cavities with everything from turpentine resin to lead. A few 18th-century dentists used gold leaf but the process did not really become widespread until the invention of dental amalgam by the Frenchman Auguste Taveau in 1816. Taveau's amalgam was created from silver and mercury, and this combination was used in fillings until very recently. Now white composite fillings

invented by the American Michael Buonocore in 1955 are the norm. Broken teeth are mended with crowns or caps. These are made either of gold or a white, porcelain-like material designed to resemble tooth enamel.

Most Americans under 40 years old have either had or know somebody who has had dental braces. These devices, designed to straighten misaligned teeth, date back earlier than you might think. The first brace designs appeared in Fauchard's 18th-century book. These consisted of a flat strip of metal tied to the teeth. Orthodontic braces have been used since 1915. These are hooks of metal attached to bands that circled the teeth. They were invented by the U.S. dentist Edward Angle. Today, clear bracket braces are available.

The other great leap forward in dentistry was the invention of false teeth, or dentures. The first people to make dentures were the Etruscans of Italy around 700 B.C.E., using human or carved animal teeth. Although dentures of this kind did not last long, they were inexpensive and were popular until the 19th century. In 1788, porcelain dentures were invented. These proved to be more durable than the natural alternative. These were improved in 1851 by the addition of close-fitting plates of vulcanite (hardened rubber) made from casts of the gums.

Regular brushing with toothpaste can keep teeth healthy for your whole life. Dental hygienists, below, give teeth a deeper cleaning.

OTHER TREATMENTS

Not all illnesses can be overcome by drugs or surgery alone. Some require extra types of treatment, or therapy. A range of therapies are available to treat injuries or help people recover after illness.

HANDS ON

Physiotherapy, osteopathy, and chiropractic are designed to alleviate problems with the muscles and joints. They are often used to treat back strains and other minor injuries, but may also provide relief from the symptoms of long-term diseases, such as arthritis. A few branches of these disciplines are highly specialized and targeted at very specific problems. Gait training, for instance, is a form of physiotherapy aimed solely at getting people to walk properly. Special equipment is used to support the upper part of the body while exercises build up strength and coordination in the legs. Chest physiotherapy is another specialized therapy. It is used to help prevent chest infections following major surgery or people who have an illness that

A podiatrist, or foot doctor, treats a patient. As well as removing corns and verrucas (fungus infections), podiatrists also make specially fitted shoes for people with damaged feet.

prevents them from clearing their lungs. Children with the inherited disorder cystic fibrosis fall into this category. Many require regular sessions of chest physiotherapy. Once the physiotherapist has the child lying down in a particular position, he or she taps the chest with cupped hands to loosen built-up mucus. Breathing and coughing exercises may also be taught to help people recover the ability to expand the chest and fill the lungs with air.

COMPLEMENTARY THERAPIES

While physiotherapy and some other forms of treatment can be used alone to treat medical conditions, there are others that add to, or complement, more established techniques. Common complementary therapies include acupuncture, hypnotherapy and homeopathy. These therapies are based on different, or alternative, ideas about medicine.

However, many complementary techniques are based on more conventional medical ideas. Biofeedback is one of these. In biofeedback therapy, body functions that are normally outside conscious control, such as skin temperature and heart rate, are recorded and played back to the patient as visual or sound signals using a computer. The patient practices breathing exercises and learns to have some control over their body functions. Essentially, he or she is taught how to calm down and relax. In time, biofeedback patients are able to enter a state of deep relaxation at will. This therapy has proved very useful for controlling panic attacks and other stress-related problems, such as insomnia and migraines. It may also help lower blood pressure and reduce joint and muscle pain.

Key inventions

Blood Transfusion

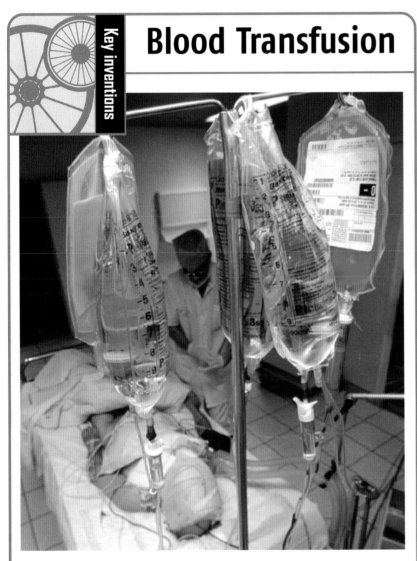

Anemia is a condition when people do not have enough hemoglobin, the red, oxygen-carrying pigment in blood cells. Severe cases of anemia are treated with blood transfusions. This involves blood from healthy individuals being transferred into sufferer's bodies by means of a narrow tube inserted directly into a vein. Blood transfusions are also given to people who have lost blood through an accident or operation (above).

HOSPITAL TREATMENTS

Some diseases require more than surgery and drugs to control or defeat them. Most cancer patients, for example, undergo radiotherapy after surgery to kill any traces of cancer that remain inside their body. High-energy radiation is produced by a machine called a linear accelerator. This has a tilting head which enables the operator to direct the radiation towards the affected area. Gamma rays, X rays, or electron beams may be used, depending on the type of cancer being treated. The first linear accelerators were introduced in the early 1950s.

Other machines may provide the same function as failed organs. Kidney dialysis machines do just this, carrying out all the roles of a healthy kidney until a donor can be found for a transplant operation.

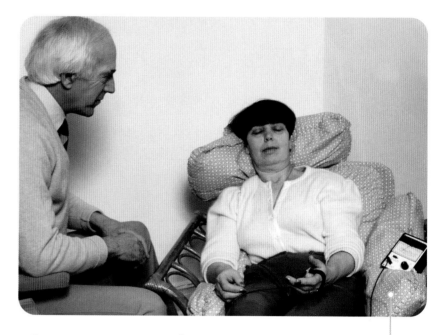

In some cases, several organs may need assistance for a person to survive. Patients in an unstable or critical condition are put into an intensive care unit. There, their breathing may be assisted using a machine called a ventilator. The heart rate is monitored using an electrocardiogram (ECG) machine and the level of oxygen

Hypnotherapy is a technique used to help people control pain or overcome an addiction. Once hypnotized the patient is given suggestions on how to deal with their problem.

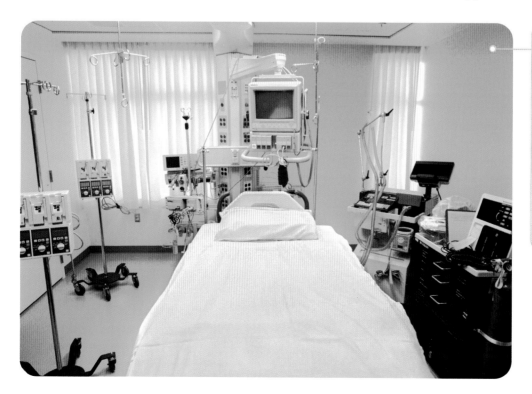

Seriously ill people are taken to the hospital's emergency room (ER). Here doctors give them the treatment they need to stay alive before sending them to another part of the hospital to recover.

Dialysis Machine

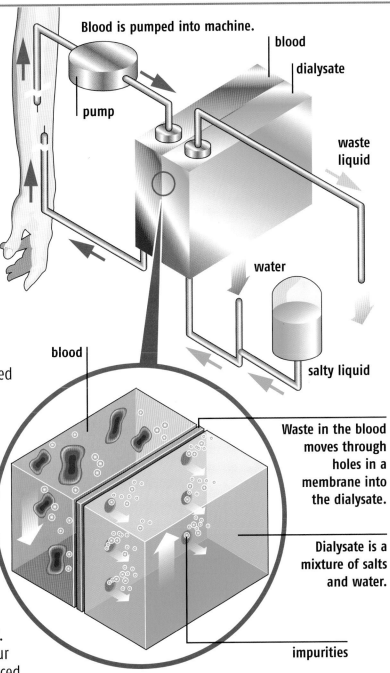

Blood is pumped into machine.

blood

dialysate

pump

waste liquid

water

blood

salty liquid

Waste in the blood moves through holes in a membrane into the dialysate.

Dialysate is a mixture of salts and water.

impurities

The kidneys are among the most important organs in the body. Their job is to filter the blood, removing the waste produced from the many chemical reactions that keep us alive. The kidneys also remove excess water from the blood. The liquid mixture they produce leaves the body as urine.

When the kidneys fail, the body becomes unable to cleanse itself. Waste products can build up to dangerous levels, leading to other problems such as high blood pressure, thin bones, and anaemia. Sudden kidney failure can even cause death.

Fortunately, failed kidneys can be treated by dialysis. This is a procedure where the normal functions of the kidney are taken over by another part of the body or a machine. In peritoneal dialysis, the membrane that surrounds the organs in the abdomen (the main trunk of the body) is used to filter the blood. This membrane, the peritoneum, has many blood vessels in it. A liquid called dialysate is injected inside the the peritoneum. Water and waste products pass from the blood vessels into the dialysate. The dialysate is then pumped out of the body and disposed of. Peritoneal dialysis must be carried out four times a day. The fresh dialysate is introduced slowly by a tube connected to a sealed bag. The tube is fitted by a doctor, so the patient just needs to plug it into the bag. The fluid remains in the body for about six hours before being drained off through another tube into a separate bag.

In haemodialysis, a kidney machine cleans the blood. Unlike peritoneal dialysis, the treatment cannot be carried out at home, but it is less frequent, usually being carried out three times a week. Blood flows through a tube from a vein directly to the machine. There it is pumped over a filter with fresh dialysate on the other side. The waste products seep into the dialysate, and the cleansed blood returns to the body. The treatment takes three to four hours.

in the blood is measured with a pulse oximeter. Other machines carry out functions that the person would do themselves if they were conscious: Liquid food is pumped directly into the stomach through a tube inserted via a nostril and suction equipment clears the airways. A drip provides the patient with fluid. This is a bag suspended above the patient. The fluid flows from the bag through a tube and enters the blood through a needle. The fluids keep the patient properly hydrated. Drugs can be administered through the drip. Intensive care has helped many people survive accidents and get through life-threatening conditions such as coma.

How things work

Radiotherapy

LEKSELL GAMMA UNIT

Following an operation to remove a cancerous tumor, many patients go through a course of radiotherapy. This treatment uses radiation to destroy any remaining cancerous cells. The radiation source may be internal or external, depending on the position of the tumor. Tumors close to the body's surface are treated with thin radioactive rods. These are inserted into the cancerous area to burn away any remaining cells.

Cancers deeper inside are treated with beams of radiation (above). Doses are kept as low as possible and carefully focused so that normal cells receive as little exposure as possible. Radiotherapy itself is painless but it does have side effects, such as temporary hair loss and nausea. It may be used alone or in combination with anticancer drugs. Treating cancers with drugs is known as chemotherapy.

Speech Therapy

Most of us take the ability to speak for granted, but we can lose it at any point in our lives. If a stroke damages the brain, for example, or a part of the throat, tongue, or face has to be removed during an operation, normal speech may become difficult or even impossible. Speech therapy is treatment to help people recover the ability to speak. It is also used to help children and adults who have always had trouble speaking. Speech problems may be as a result of learning difficulties, a stammer, or a physical problem such as impaired hearing or a cleft palate.

The approach used in speech therapy varies according to the nature of the problem. Children may be encouraged to play games that involve verbal description (above). Adults who have a problem articulating words following an accident or operation might be given physical exercises to strengthen the muscles used in speech. Brain damage caused by a stroke may result in problems

with remembering the right words for things. This can be overcome by repeated mental exercises, such as describing objects in pictures.

In some cases, speech therapy needs a helping hand from technology. For example, removal of part or all of the larynx (voice box) to treat cancer will result in the loss of normal speech altogether. Patients can be taught to speak again by slowly releasing air from the esophagus (the tube leading from the back of the mouth to the stomach). But this burping technique is often too quiet to hear. A person's voice can be replaced with an electric voice aid. This aid makes a buzzing noise and is held against the neck. The user mouths the words as normal and can speak relatively clearly.

Alternatively, the patient might have an operation to fit a tracheoesophageal implant. Placed between the esophagus and the windpipe, this device uses inhaled air to produce sound that can be converted into speech by using the teeth, lips, and tongue.

MUSCLE DAMAGE

Healing damaged muscles and ligaments after an operation or injury takes time. In order to speed recovery, doctors often refer patients to a physical therapist or another medical professional who specializes in restoring strength and flexibility to muscles. As well as helping people recover, physiotherapy can be used to relieve pain and prevent complications arising after illness or an operation. It can also help people with progressive disorders, such as cystic fibrosis, to keep their bodies working normally for longer.

A visit to the physical therapist begins with a series of questions to establish the patient's medical history. After that, the patient may be asked to bend and stretch a little, in order for the physical therapist to evaluate the flexibility and strength of their muscles. Once the physical therapist has identified the severity of the problem, he or she will draw up a treatment plan. This will include one or more of the following techniques: exercise, massage, heat and cold, electrical stimulation, ultrasound, and hydrotherapy.

Physiotherapists help people recover from injury. They teach them several exercises that strengthen damaged muscles.

Exercise is usually used for strengthening weak muscles following a long period of disuse because of injury or confinement to bed. The physical therapist may prescribe exercises for the patient to perform or manipulate a limb or joint to help extend the range of its movement. Prescribed exercises may include the use of equipment such as weights or a treadmill. Exercise is an important part of gait training—helping a person recover the ability to walk, through physiotherapy, after illness or injury.

Massage helps reduce inflammation by stimulating blood flow and may also remove some fluid from the affected area. It is practiced by kneading muscles with the hands or specialized massage tools. Physical therapists sometimes use massage just to relieve tension and promote relaxation. This can help relieve muscle spasm and soothe away pain.

Heat and cold treatments are exactly as they sound. Hot packs are placed on areas of injury or stiffness to improve blood flow, relieve pain, and relax muscle tension. Ice packs may be used on injured muscles or arthritic joints to reduce swelling and pain.

Electrical stimulation and ultrasound are really just variations on the principle of heat treatment. In the first one, pads applied to the skin have a mild electric current passed through them to generate heat in muscles, tendons, or ligaments. In the second, high energy sound waves are used to create warmth in the tissues.

Hydrotherapy is the use of water to support the body in order to help with exercise.

People unable to bear the weight on an injured or diseased limb often find hydrotherapy useful because the water takes their weight. They can perform useful exercises in water that would not be possible out of it.

Physiotherapy uses all of these techniques. But other disciplines treat damaged muscle in other ways. Osteopathy and chiropractic are two different forms of "manipulative therapy," where muscles and bone are moved to relieve pain.

Both osteopathy and chiropractic are very useful for treating back pain. Chiropractors concentrate on realigning the vertebrae (bones of the spine) to achieve the desired result. The bones are manipulated using precise, sharp hand movements. Osteopaths use similar methods but may also manipulate the limbs.

Chiropractors and osteopaths move the body in very controlled ways. This relaxes muscles and realigns damaged joints.

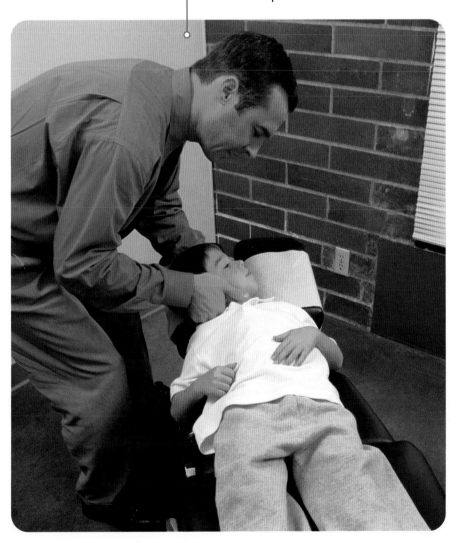

HELPING NEW LIFE

It was many years before women were able to practice medicine on an equal basis with men. The first female American doctor was Elizabeth Blackwell. She was only licensed in New York in 1849. However, women had always had an important role in all areas of medicine. Women nursed sick loved ones at home before the development of hospitals. In ancient times, the majority of female health workers were midwives, who helped pregnant women give birth to their babies. Doctors have only become fully involved in childbirth in the last few centuries. Today most midwives are still women, although more men are becoming involved. They perform the same role as they have done for thousands of years, but can get help from specialist doctors—both male and female— called obstetricians when needed.

PREGNANCY AND BIRTH
Until the early 20th century, birth was a very dangerous event. Records show that in the United States in the 1920s, more than 17 percent of women died during or soon after childbirth. The reasons for this high figure ranged from poor hygiene to problems caused by inexperienced doctors. In modern time prenatal (before-birth) care of pregnant women

A nurse-midwife holds a newborn baby. As well as helping before and during the birth, midwives also help new mothers look after their children in the first few weeks of their life.

Reproductive Genetics

Making a baby requires material from both the mother and the father. This is why children often grow up looking like both of their parents. The mother provides one ovum, or egg cell, and the father a single sperm. Each of these contains half of the genetic material needed to make a new person. The egg and sperm fuse to make a single zygote cell. This first cell begins to divide and grows into an embryo. After nine months the embryo has grown into a fully developed baby.

Like all human cells, the zygote contains 46 chromosomes: 23 of these come from the mother's egg, the other 23 are from the sperm. The chromosomes contain deoxyribonucleic acid (DNA). This is an extremely long molecule that determines how cells in the body grow and work. In essence, it is like a book of code, with different sections coding for different features and functions.

The DNA molecule is made up of components called bases, which pair up to form what look like rungs in a spiraling ladder, or double helix. There are four types of bases. The order that they are arranged is what makes up the code. A section of DNA that codes for one specific feature or function is known as a gene. The field of inheritance is called genetics.

The way that ova and sperm cells are produced means that the DNA in every one of them is unique. This is why no two people are the same. It is shared by no one else. One exception to this rule, of course, is identical twins. They do have the same DNA as each other because they were formed from the same fertilized egg. Identical twins grow in the womb when a fertilized egg splits early in its development. Non-identical twins grow from two separate fertilized eggs.

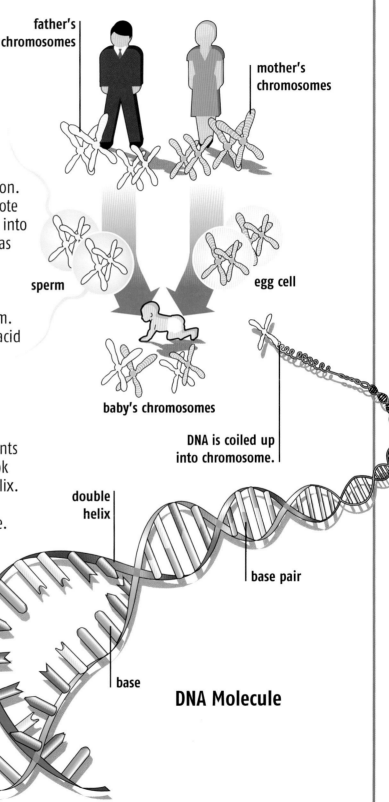

father's chromosomes

mother's chromosomes

sperm

egg cell

baby's chromosomes

DNA is coiled up into chromosome.

double helix

base pair

base

DNA Molecule

Born Too Soon

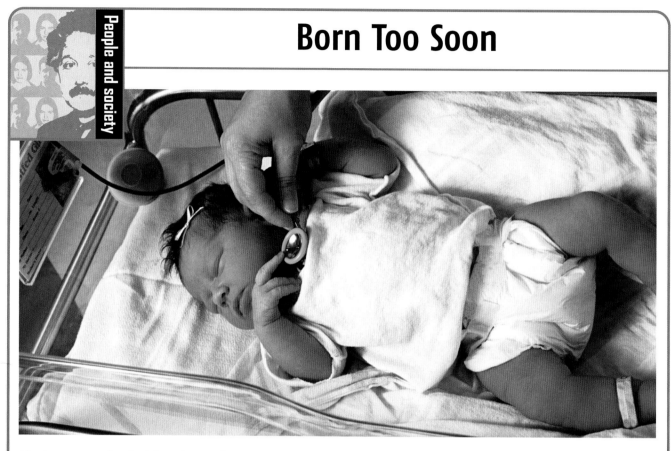

Most pregnancies last for about nine months. This is the time it takes for an unborn baby to develop completely. A pregnancy that reaches nine months is said to have been full term. Babies born more than three weeks before the full term is reached are known as preterm, or premature, babies. In the past, few very premature babies lived for long after they were born. But with today's specialist care, even babies born as early as five months have a chance of survival.

Preterm babies suffer from a number of problems that full term babies do not. With their smaller size, thin skin, and lack of fat, premature children lose heat much more easily. They may also have trouble breathing properly because their lungs are underdeveloped. And they are more prone to infection than babies born later.

With proper care, however, most of these problems can be overcome or avoided. Modern care ensures that most babies born after six and a half months not only survive, but grow up normally without any continuing medical problems. All preterm babies must be kept warm and fed very often. Many need no more treatment than that.

As soon as most preterm babies are born, they are transferred to an incubator. These machines (above) have been used since 1894. They are heated to keep the child warm enough so it can continue its development. The incubator may also be equipped with machines that monitor the baby. The baby spends most of its time in the incubator, under the watchful eyes of medical staff, until it grows big enough to be cared for by its mother.

Babies that are too young to feed naturally are provided with the nutrients using a drip into the bloodstream or via a tube passed through the nose into the stomach. Those with breathing problems may also be put on a ventilator. This provides both oxygen and a vital substance called surfactant, which is absent in premature babies but produced by fully developed lungs.

Fact Premature births occur for a number of reasons. There is often a problem with the placenta, the organ that links the developing fetus to the mother. Drugs are used to stop premature births from happening.

and their unborn babies and a better understanding of labor has helped to reduce this figure.

Today's expectant mothers are kept well informed about the health of the fetus (unborn child) growing inside them. Ultrasound is used to make live images of the developing baby. However, techniques for monitoring fetal development were slow to emerge. In 1828, the French obstetrician Adolphe Pinard (1794–1897) invented a stethoscope that could detect the heartbeats of unborn babies. He also developed a massage technique for turning babies around in the womb so that they would be born head-first—the safest position. In 1916, the Norwegian Christian Kielland (1871–1941) developed a new design of forceps (scooped tongs) for pulling on a baby's head during a difficult birth. However, in untrained hands these were a danger to baby and mother alike, and they often caused more problems than they solved.

Slowly though, the hazards of childbirth began to be removed. Blood transfusions and drugs began to save lives from the 1930s. Painkillers such as morphine made labor easier. Between the 1930s and the 1980s, better ways of giving pain relief were developed. An epidural involves

Many expectant parents attend prenatal classes. They learn what their babies are doing inside the mother, and are given advice on how to prepare for the birth and how to look after their child.

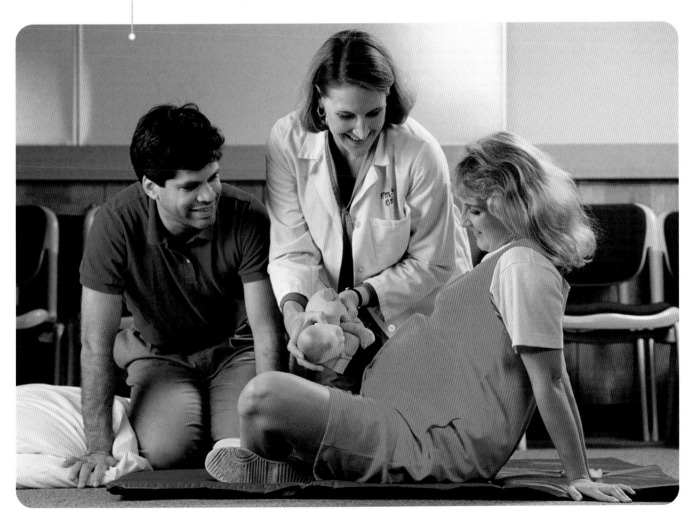

injecting a numbing anesthetic into the back around the spinal cord. This blocks any pain signals from below the injection reaching the brain. Epidurals are used to help women tired out from a long, difficult labor. They are even given before emergency Caesarean sections. A Caesarean section is an incision made in a mother's belly to remove a baby that cannot be born in the normal way.

MODERN DEVELOPMENTS

Today women have a lot of control over when they have children. Contraception allows them to decide when they become pregnant. New technology has made it easier for infertile people, who cannot have children naturally, to become parents. The most used fertility treatment is in-vitro fertilization (IVF), which was

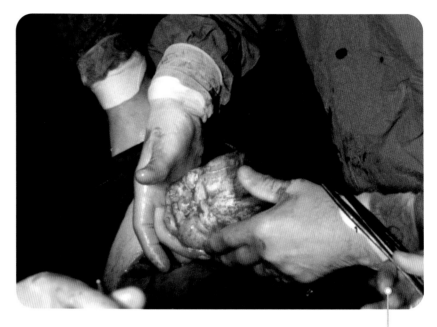

developed in the late 1970s. Children born using IVF became known as test-tube babies, even though test-tubes were never actually involved in the process. Today, there are many thousands of test-tube babies. The world's first test-tube baby, Louise Brown, was born in Britain in 1978.

A surgeon delivers a baby by Caesarean section. This procedure is necessary when the baby is in the wrong position in the mother's uterus. It is called a Caesarean for Roman emperor Julius Caesar who was born this way.

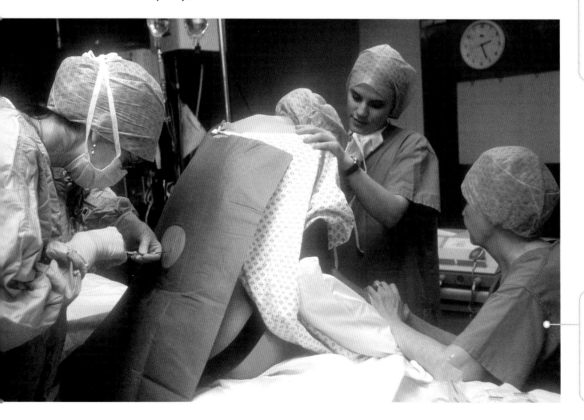

An anesthesiologist injects drugs into a woman's spine. This will numb her lower body during labor.

Contraception

How things work

Babies are formed by sexual intercourse between a man and a woman, but there are many ways of preventing this process from resulting in a pregnancy. All that is required is that the man's sperm and the woman's egg do not meet, or, if they do, that the fertilized egg does not implant in the wall of the uterus (womb) and grow into a baby.

One way of preventing sperm and egg from meeting is for the man or woman to wear a rubber sheath called a condom (1). Condoms have the added advantage of acting as barriers to sexually transmitted diseases. A cap, or diaphragm, worn by a woman, also work by blocking the sperm. They do not prevent the spread of sexually transmitted diseases, however. Intrauterine devices (IUDs, or coils) are placed inside women's uteruses. They make it harder for fertilized eggs to continue developing.

Alternatively, either sex could be sterilized. In men, this procedure involves cutting the vas deferens. These tubes carry sperm from the testes, where they are produced. Women are sterilized by having their oviducts cut or tied. These tubes link the ovaries, where eggs are made, to the uterus.

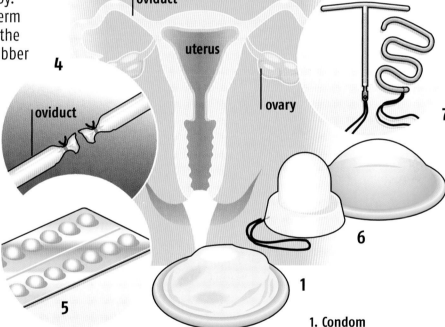

vas deferens

testis

oviduct

uterus

ovary

oviduct

Since it became available in the 1960s, the "pil"l has become the most used form of contraception. Taken by the woman, it prevents her from releasing eggs in the first place. A pill that stops men producing sperm has been developed but is not widely available. There are concerns over whether men would use it properly.

1. Condom

2. Male sterilization

3. Male pill

4. Female sterilization

5. Female pill

6. Diaphragm

7. Intrauterine device

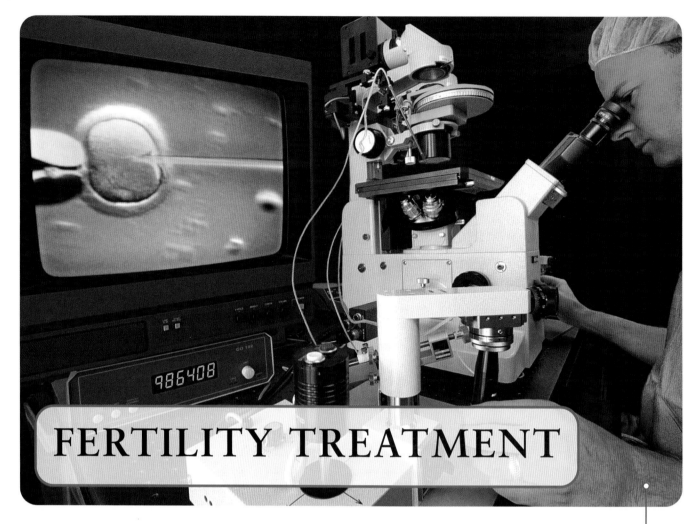

FERTILITY TREATMENT

A technician looks at an egg with a microscope. He is injecting the egg with DNA from a sperm during fertility treatment.

Some couples have trouble making a baby. There are a number of reasons why this may be the case. The woman's oviducts may be damaged or blocked, meaning that her eggs are unable to travel from her ovaries to her uterus. She might suffer from a condition that prevents her ovulating (releasing an egg from the ovary) normally. Or she may produce antibodies in the mucus of her cervix. The cervix is the link between the uterus and the vagina. The cervical antibodies are substances that destroy her partner's sperms. If the lining of the uterus is

damaged or infected fertilized eggs cannot implant in it and continue developing.

Inability to conceive (make a baby) is not always the issue of the woman, however. In almost one in three couples that experience difficulties, the problem stems from the man. Often it is simply a matter of the man not producing enough sperm cells to ensure that one will reach the egg. A low sperm count may be caused by a number of factors, many of which can be easily rectified. For example, smoking, alcohol, and tight clothing

can all impair the production of sperms. Sperms may be damaged rather than just low in number, and be unable to travel to the egg. In these cases, doctors remove the DNA from a sperm and inject it directly into an egg.

Other fertility treatment makes use of manufactured hormones to improve the chances of a couple producing a healthy baby. Women may receive this treatment to encourage ovulation. Less commonly, men may have hormone treatment to boost sperm production.

The synthetic hormones used include gonadorelin (for men and women) and anti-estrogens such as clomifene (for women only). These drugs jump-start processes in the body that would normally be triggered by natural hormones, which are either absent from the patient's body or occur in insufficient quantities to do the job.

In-vitro fertilization (IVF) is a treatment that helps couples who are unable to bring sperms and eggs together naturally, for any of the reasons already described. *In-vitro* means literally "in glass," and the IVF process allows babies to be conceived outside of the woman's body.

Early in her menstrual cycle, the woman is injected with fertility drugs to encourage her ovaries to produce many more eggs than usual. Over the following days and weeks, ultrasound scans are used to monitor the ripening of these eggs in her ovaries. Then, just before ovulation, the ripe eggs are removed from one ovary using a long, hollow needle. These are transferred to a glass dish, where they are fertilized with the male partner's sperms. Over the next few days, the fertilized eggs divide and become tiny embryos. These are inserted into the woman's uterus where, with luck, one or more will grow into a baby.

While IVF works for many couples, some women are unable to have a baby because their uterus is too damaged. Couples with this problem can still have a baby by using a surrogate mother. The woman goes through the same process she would if she were having IVF. However, at the last stage, her embryos are implanted into another woman's uterus. This woman gives birth to the child and reunites it with the parents.

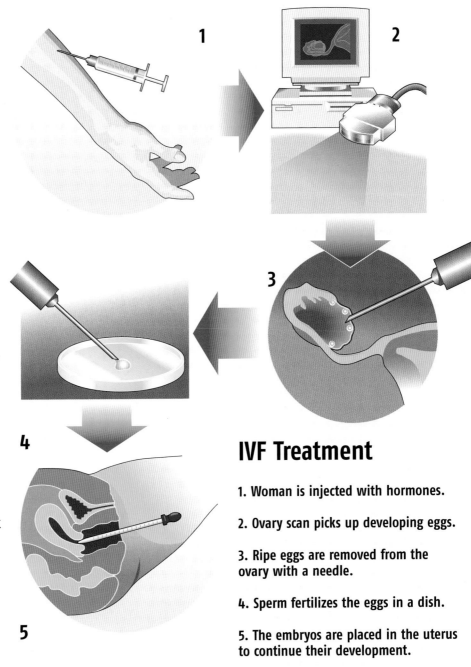

IVF Treatment

1. Woman is injected with hormones.

2. Ovary scan picks up developing eggs.

3. Ripe eggs are removed from the ovary with a needle.

4. Sperm fertilizes the eggs in a dish.

5. The embryos are placed in the uterus to continue their development.

DISABILITY

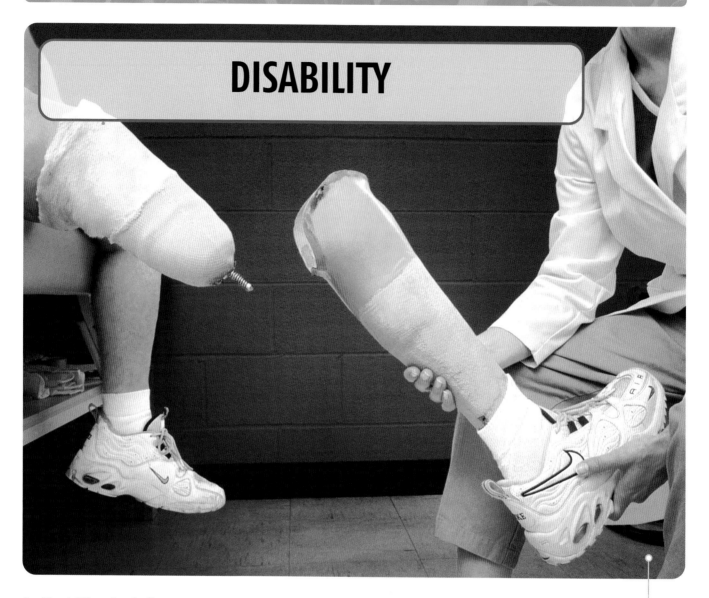

A prosthetic (artificial) leg is fitted to a person's calf. This leg has been made to fit the patient exactly. It replaces a leg that has been removed, or amputated, after an accident.

A disability is defined as a condition that affects a person's physical or mental capabilities. It may be caused by injury or present from birth. People with a disability might be unable to walk, see, or reason as well as most others. Usually, a disabled person will have just a single disability, but occasionally they might have more than one.

PHYSICAL DISABILITY

Physical disability affects one in every 30 people at some point during their lives. It may range from the loss of one of the senses, such as hearing, to a reduction in the ability to coordinate the hands or to walk. The causes are varied. Blindness, for example, might be congenital (present from birth) or be the result of an injury or illness.

Dealing with disability is not a new field of medicine. In fact, physical disability caused by illness is less common than it once used to be. Several diseases, such as poliomyelitis and leprosy would disable sufferers until relatively recently. Poliomyelitis,

Alzheimer's Disease

Alzheimer's disease is a wasting disease of the brain, characterized by a gradual loss of memory, concentration, and ability to understand language. It can affect anybody but usually sets in late in life. Most people who develop the illness are over the age of 65. Alzheimer's disease is a distressing condition for patient and family alike. After several years, sufferers (above) are often unable to recognize close friends or relatives. Long-term sufferers become unable to look after themselves and usually require full-time care. Eventually the brain becomes so damaged the sufferer is unable to swallow food. They become weak and susceptible to illness, which eventually kills them. The disease is named for Alois Alzheimer, who first described the brain disorder in 1907.

Wheelchairs

For most people who are unable to walk, the wheelchair provides the main means of getting around. Today's wheelchairs vary from basic folding models to sleek three-wheelers designed for racing (above). Motorization means that just about anybody can get about independently, no matter how frail they are. There are even off-road wheelchairs for traveling over rough terrain.

People have been using wheelchairs for many hundreds of years. The oldest evidence comes from China, where an engraving made in 525 c.e. shows a man being pushed in a chair with three wheels. Outside China, wheeled chairs did not appear until the 16th century. The most famous wheelchair user of that time was King Phillip II of Spain, who suffered from a type of arthritis. In 1595, the king had an adjustable chair with wheels and foot rests made to keep him mobile.

The first record of a self-propelled chair dates back to 1655, when Stephen Farfler, a German watchmaker who had both legs amputated, built himself a wheelchair he could power with his hands. The chair resembled a tricycle with the front wheel driven by a cog. The cog was turned with handles rather than pedals.

Large-scale production of wheelchairs began in the late 18th century. In 1783, an Englishman named John Dawson invented the Bath chair, which was named for the British city where he lived. Built for outdoor use, the Bath chair had three wheels, a hood, and a wooden door that closed to cover the legs. Dawson's design dominated throughout the 19th century. In 1875, it was updated and made more comfortable by adding hollow rubber tires.

Wheelchairs resembling those we see today first appeared in 1932, when the Americans Herbert Everest and Harry Jennings designed a metal wheelchair that could be folded up and put in a car trunk. The first commercially available electric wheelchair was designed and built in 1956 by the same people. By that time, Everest and Jennings were heading up their own company, which dominated the wheelchair market.

able to do something about them. Prostheses (artificial body parts), for instance, have been with us for thousands of years. The earliest record of a prosthesis comes from India about 5,000 years ago. It tells of how the warrior queen Vishpla lost her leg in battle and then had an iron replacement fitted so that she could fight again.

Prostheses may have been more common in the past than surviving evidence suggests, since most people did not leave records of their lives. By the late Middle Ages, artificial limbs had become quite complex and were capable of various movements. Frequently, people involved in making suits of armor also made iron prostheses.

Other aids to mobility have been around for just as long, if not longer, than artificial limbs. The Bible, for example, mentions several walking aids. A man using a crutch appears on the entrance to an ancient Egyptian tomb built around 2830 B.C.E. Wheelchairs also have a long history, dating back more than 1,000 years.

SENSORY DISABILITY

Not all physical disabilities impact on mobility, some affect the senses such as sight and hearing. Until quite recently, all forms of blindness and deafness were untreatable. Thankfully, that situation has now changed, and in many cases vision and hearing can be completely restored. For example, electronic hearing aids,

This person has cerebral palsy. This brain disease makes it hard for her to control muscle movements. This motorized chair makes her mobile. It is controlled by a keyboard.

or polio is a virus that causes paralysis, especially in children. The disease has been all but eradicated in most parts of the world. So has leprosy, a bacterial infection that causes nerve damage and physical disfigurement.

In the past, most people had to just live with their handicaps untreated. A few however were first invented in 1898, have brought sound back into the lives of millions of people. New surgical techniques have been developed to cure several causes of blindness. In the future, blindness may be eliminated forever. Electronic technology may soon be able to help the brain convert light signals into a visual image.

MENTAL DISABILITY

The mentally disabled are generally considered to be individuals with abnormally low mental ability. Many of these people do not require special medical attention, since they are able to look after themselves from day to day. However, they are often more vulnerable to danger than other adults.

A person's intelligence is expressed as their intelligence quotient (IQ). IQ is calculated using written and visual tests. The average IQ at each age is 100. People with an IQ of less than 70 are considered to be mentally disabled.

Deaf children are taught to communicate with sign language. Sign language can be used to spell out words like names, but more common words have their own particular sign.

Deafness

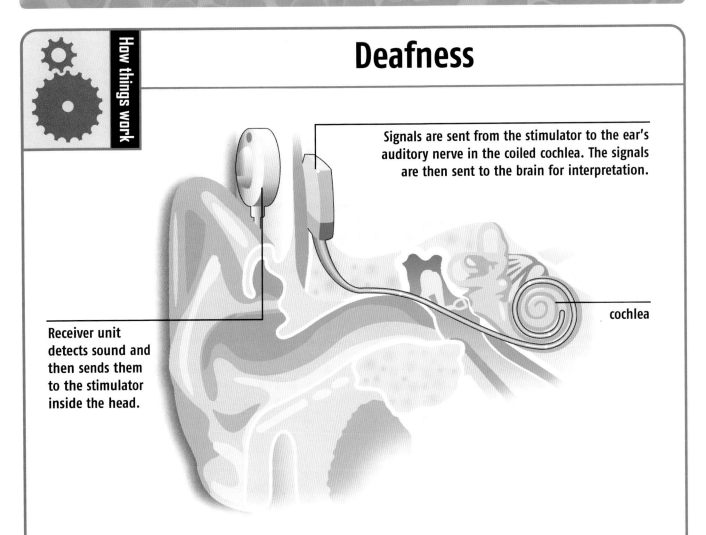

Signals are sent from the stimulator to the ear's auditory nerve in the coiled cochlea. The signals are then sent to the brain for interpretation.

cochlea

Receiver unit detects sound and then sends them to the stimulator inside the head.

Most people with normal hearing imagine that people who are deaf cannot hear anything at all. In fact, this is generally not the case. A complete inability to hear, or profound deafness, affects only a small minority of deaf people. The majority have either conductive or sensori-neural hearing loss. Both of these disorders allow at least some types of sound to be heard.

Conductive hearing loss is caused by sound being unable to pass normally from the outer to the inner ear. This may be either the result of blockage or damage to the middle ear. Conductive hearing loss causes all sounds to be heard much more quietly. Loud voices sound like whispers, while soft voices may not be heard at all.

Sensori-neural hearing loss is the result of damage to the inner ear and causes sounds to become distorted. Although less common than conductive hearing loss, it is more likely to be permanent. In most cases of sensori-neural

hearing loss, high-frequency sounds are cut out. The result is that the vowels in speech are audible but most consonants are not.

Hearing aids benefit people with conductive hearing loss. These tiny devices that fit in the ear work like miniature amplifiers, making quiet sounds louder to cancel out the effect of middle ear damage. People with sensori-neural hearing loss and the profoundly deaf cannot use hearing aids like this. However, they may have a cochlear implant (above) fitted. This small device is surgically implanted into the inner ear. A computer unit fitted behind the outer ear converts sounds into a simplified sound signal, which is transmitted into the head.

★ Fact Deaf people can learn to talk, but because they cannot hear their own voice, they may sound odd. Many also lip-read, figuring out what is said by watching the mouth.

ALTERNATIVE MEDICINE

MENTAL ILLNESS

The scan of the head of a person with schizophrenia shows the varying level of activity in different areas of the brain.

Mental health problems strike one in four people at some point during their lives. They vary from phobias and depression to severe personality disorders. Most mental illnesses can be treated. Unfortunately, many sufferers are embarrassed or refuse to admit that they have a problem. This means that many people suffering with mental illness never seek help and so go untreated.

A common mental illness is depression. Doctors estimate that one in ten people suffer from it at one time or another. Depression is characterized by suicidal feelings. The causes are varied but often linked to stress or a sudden, traumatic event, such as the death of a loved one. New mothers may suffer from what is known as post-partum depression. The arrival of a baby can bring feelings of helplessness and a loss of self-esteem. Physical diseases, including hormonal disorders and some infections can lead to depression. The condition may even arise as a side effect of certain drugs, such as beta-blockers used to control heart disorders.

Doctors treat depression with drugs. They arrange for patients to see a psychologist, who will use cognitive therapy to help the patients understand their negative feelings and control them.

Other mental illnesses include bipolar affective disorder, phobias, and schizophrenia. Bipolar affective disorder is also known as manic depression. Sufferers go through bouts of abnormally high levels of activity (mania) followed by periods of depression. Bipolar affective disorder may recur at various points in a person's life. The symptoms can be controlled with drugs, but some sufferers may need to be admitted to a hospital. Psychiatrists (mind doctors) treat manic depressives with drugs and counseling. Extreme cases might be dealt with by electroshock therapy. This involves passing electricity through the brain.

Phobias are irrational fears that are so extreme they affect a person's life. Most are treated by desensitization therapy. In this, the sufferer is gradually introduced to the object of their fear. Somebody with arachnophobia might first be shown a picture of a spider, for example, before eventually gaining enough confidence to touch a real, live specimen.

A psychiatrist talks to a patient. Psychiatrists are doctors and can prescribe drugs to their patient, but they may also try a "talking cure," in which they help the patient understand their illness better. This idea has been developed from the work of Sigmund Freud.

Schizophrenia and other personality disorders are much more serious mental illnesses. A schizophrenic's sense of reality is different from other people's. They do not have split personalities, as is often believed, but may hear strange voices and feel persecuted. Drugs ease the condition and one in five sufferers makes a full recovery.

Personality disorders affect an individual's ability to fit in with society. Psychopaths and sociopaths, for example, lack any feelings for other people. They may display extremely disturbing behavior without any rational reasons.

ALTERNATIVE MEDICINE

Many people believe that crystals can cure disease. Crystals are ordered solids, which can be made to vibrate. Quartz, used to keep time in electric clocks, for example, is a crystal that vibrates at a fixed rate. Although it has not been proven, crystal therapy is supposed to use vibrations to change the flow of energy through a diseased body.

Alternative medicine includes all forms of medicine provided today that have not been researched and proven by scientific methods. It is a broad spectrum of ideas containing everything from herbalism to faith healing. Many forms of alternative medicine appear to work, although it is not understood how. Some others, however, have been shown to have little or no medical benefit.

HERBALISM

Before the application of science to medicine from the 18th century, herbal remedies made up the bulk of treatments available to people for illness. Herbalism continues that tradition today. The many treatments it offers are all prepared from natural plant ingredients. Many herbal remedies are based on recipes that have remained unchanged for many hundreds of years.

Probably the most widely used form of alternative medicine today, herbalism has several branches. Some herbalists offer remedies drawn from a variety of different cultures and traditions. They include medieval European treatments from more than a

People and society

Echinacea

In the western world, echinacea is probably the best known of all herbal remedies. Unlike the majority of herbal treatments, which can only be purchased from speciality stores, it can be bought in most drugstores and even many supermarkets.

Echinacea is the Latin name of a wild flower growing in the Midwest. It was first used by the Comanche and Sioux peoples, who chewed its leaves (left) to make a compress for snake bites and cuts. According to them, it prevented infection, and by the 1800s it had begun to appear in the medicine cabinets of American settlers.

As time passed, the use of echinacea spread throughout the United States. Then, in the late 20th century, capsules, drops, and other forms of herbal medicine made from the plant started to become popular in Europe and Australia, too. Today, the production and sale of echinacea products has become a multi-million dollar industry. Most of these products sell on the promise that they protect against the common colds and flu, yet clinical trials to test this claim have so far found them to be ineffective.

Faith Healing

There have been faith healers for almost as long as there have been people with medical problems. Throughout history, many faith healers have also doubled as priests, tribal shamans, or spiritual guides.

Faith healing is normally based on religious belief. The healer drives out demons, offers blessings, or acts as a channel to a supernatural being. Ill people are told that if they believe strongly enough, they can be cured. Faith healing remains common today. People who claim to offer it range from evangelical ministers to individuals who call themselves spiritual readers or psychics (left).

The Christian Scientists are perhaps the largest group of faith healers in the United States. This sect believes that, among other things, disease is caused by a denial of the true nature of God. Jesus Christ, they say, healed the sick by revealing this true nature to them. Christian Scientists believe they will return to full health once they fully understand this.

To date, there has been no scientific study that shows that faith healing has any effect on disease at all. There have, however, been several exposures of faith-healing scams.

thousand years ago. These include yarrow leaf tea, used for reducing fever, and camomile tea, which is said to help control headaches. Ayurvedic medicine, which arose in India about four thousand years ago is also becoming increasingly popular.

Perhaps the most established form of herbalism is that which is used within Chinese medicine. Chinese medicine is used by vast numbers of people in the country where it originated, and it is now available in most parts of the

world. Although some Chinese remedies use animal ingredients, most are made from plants. It is these that are most popular in the western world. Many herbalists today offer a range of Chinese remedies, including aconite for pain relief and ginseng for a wide variety of ailments.

HOMEOPATHY

Homeopathy is closely allied to herbalism. Natural substances that cause the symptoms of a disease are introduced into the body in

A homeopathic remedy is prepared. Active ingredients are chosen not because they reduce symptoms, like many conventional drugs do, but because they actually cause them. For example, since an onion produces a runny nose and watery eyes, it is used to treat a cold. Active ingredients are diluted with water before being taken. Some remedies are so diluted that it is impossible for all the doses to contain even one molecule of the ingredient.

Acupuncture

An important part of Chinese medicine, acupuncture has been used in East Asia for centuries. Long, thin needles are inserted at various points, known as acupoints on the body in order to relieve pain, fatigue, or symptoms of an illness.

The process by which acupuncture works is mysterious. So far nobody has come up with a satisfactory scientific theory to explain it. According to the ancient Chinese theory on which acupuncture is based, it frees up the flow of Qi between different parts of the body. *Qi* is pronounced "chy", and means "energy." Acupoints are arranged on lines called meridians (right). Qi moves around the body via these meridians. The needles are used by the acupuncturist to release, boost, or block the flow of Qi.

In recent decades, acupuncture has become increasingly popular in North America. Statistics suggest that one in ten American adults has tried it. Many people who have received acupuncture attest to its effectiveness. Many family doctors suggest their patients try it, and it is even recommended by the World Health Organization for more than 40 different medical conditions, from blocked noses to back pain. In China it remains an integral part of everyday healthcare.

 Medical researchers have shown that acupuncture increases the level of endorphins in the brain. Endorphins are natural painkillers that work like morphine.

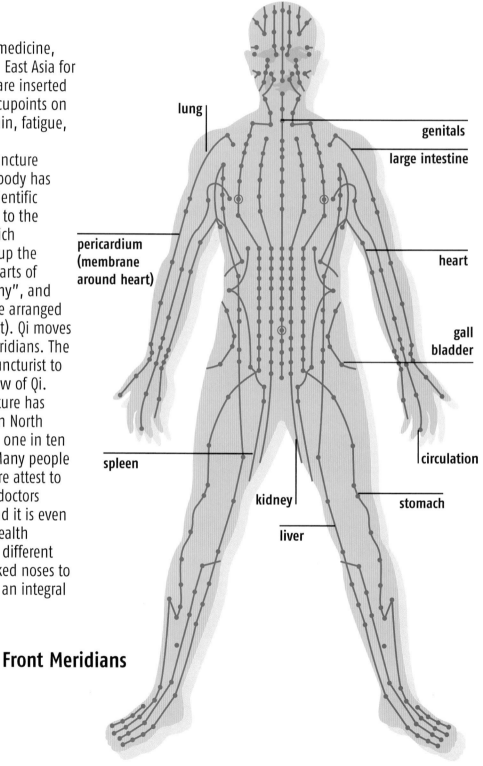

lung

genitals

large intestine

pericardium (membrane around heart)

heart

gall bladder

circulation

spleen

stomach

kidney

liver

Front Meridians

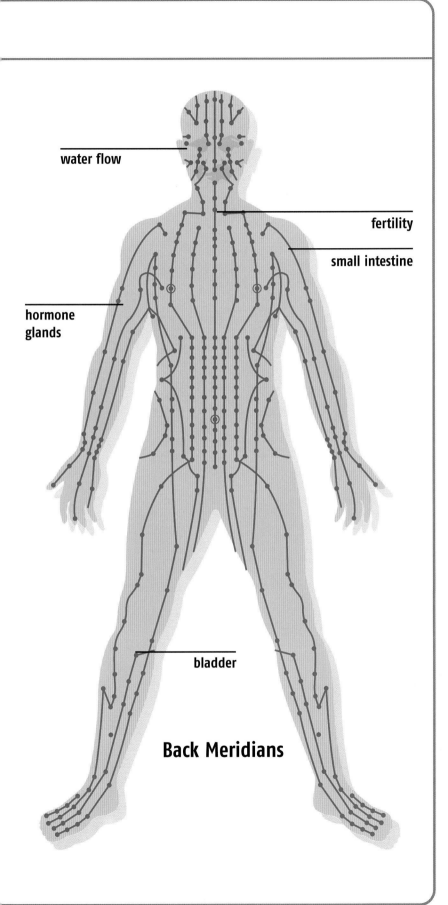

water flow

fertility

small intestine

hormone glands

bladder

Back Meridians

tiny quantities. The aim is to boost the immune system's ability to defend against the cause of the disease itself. Whether or not homeopathy works is debatable, but it certainly does no harm. The doses used are so tiny they cannot be dangerous. The worst result is when they just have no effect at all.

Homeopathy has been practiced for more than 200 years. The concept was originated by a German doctor called Samuel Hahnemann (1755–1843). He used it to treat plague victims in Leipzig during the 1800s. Almost 200 of Hahnemann's patients survived, leading to widespread recognition of his new type of treatment. During World War II (1939–45), several units of U.S. Army soldiers were treated homeopathically for flu. Again, the results appeared to be successful. Soldiers treated recovered faster than those who simply rode the illness out.

Homeopathic remedies are prepared by a process of repeated dilution, so that the final product contains a tiny quantity of the active ingredients, if any at all. Homeopaths believe that the more diluted a preparation is, the more potent it becomes. Exactly how this can be the case is not understood. Nevertheless, this form of medicine is gaining popularity across the world.

The ingredients of remedies include minerals, such as calcium, plant products, and occasionally animal extracts, such as the venom in wasp stings. They are normally administered in liquid or pill form over a period of several days.

HYPNOTHERAPY

Although classed as an alternative medicine, many doctors accept hypnotherapy as a useful tool for tackling behavioral problems. Hypnosis causes patients to enter a trancelike state in which they are more susceptible to sensible suggestions than when fully awake. Hypnotherapists can take advantage of this by proposing positive ideas that help patients change their problem behaviors.

Hypnosis as we know it has existed since the 18th century. It was first practiced by the German Franz Anton Mesmer (1734–1815), who gave his name to the modern word *mesmerize*. Mesmer used his talent to cure psychological problems and included many important people among his clients. Unfortunately, in 1785, after moving to Paris, Mesmer was banned from practicing by the French authorities.

Today, hypnotherapy is enjoying a revival. It has a high success rate in helping people quit smoking. Many hypnotherapists are now medically qualified.

A woman has herbal oil dripped on to her head in an ayurvedic treatment in Sri Lanka. The oil will be massaged into the head to wash away toxins and restore a healthy balance of energy in the body.

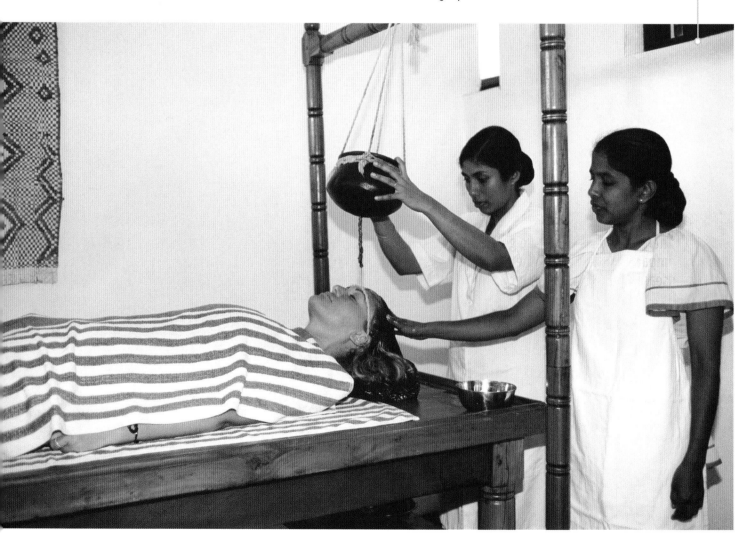

Ethnobotany

Ethnobotany is the study of the ways the world's different peoples use plants. Its application is particularly important to the development of new medicinal drugs. Over the years, ethnobotanists have turned up plants that have gone on to have a huge impact on health and the treatment of many diseases. For example, after it was found being used medicinally by local people, the rosy periwinkle of Madagascar was collected by ethnobotanists for use in research. Two substances produced by the rosy periwinkle, called vincristine and vinblastine, have since been found to have powerful anti-cancer properties. They are now used in chemotherapy against various tumors.

Ethnobotany is a relatively new scientific discipline. The name was thought up in 1896 by the American botanist John Harshburger to describe what he saw as a new practice—obtaining traditional knowledge about plants from the world's people. However, the roots of ethnobotany go back much further than its official history might suggest. In the 16th century Spanish explorers learned that South American people chewed the bark of the cinchona tree to fight the symptoms of malaria. The Europeans began using the bark themselves. Before long, it was being sent back to Europe, where it was used to treat different fevers. Later, the active ingredient of the bark, quinine, was isolated by chemists. This drug is still the most powerful antimalarial treatment today.

Towards the end of the 20th century, ethnobotany expanded as pharmaceutical (drug) companies began to take a greater interest in it. Some of them now have teams of ethnobotanists working around the world. They visit village elders or go to traditional medicine shops, such as the one above in South Africa, to learn about the ingredients used in remedies.

CHINESE MEDICINE

The tradition of what we now call conventional medicine has its roots in European and Middle Eastern history. The ancient Greek Hippocrates and the Roman Galen gave way to the work of Arab doctor Ibn-Sina and the English doctor William Harvey. Eventually, a type of medicine based on science developed in the 19th century. As Europeans spread across the world, this form of medicine was spread with them. It is now the accepted wisdom across much of the globe. But there were other schools of medical thought, most notably in China.

Today, China is home to almost a quarter of the world's population. Five times as many people live there as in the United States. Even now, most people in China trust in their traditional medicine, which includes many techniques and cures very unlike those in the West.

Chinese medicine has a history that stretches back to long before Hippocrates was born in 460 B.C.E. The earliest evidence comes from so-called "oracle bones." These were tablets containing inscriptions detailing illnesses, medicines, and treatments. These bones

Seahorses are used in Chinese remedies. Many species of seahorse, and other animals used in Chinese medicine have become very rare.

date from the Shang Dynasty (1766–1122 B.C.E.), the first period of China's history. Later evidence includes detailed medical accounts written on silk and bamboo from the first century C.E.

Modern Chinese medicine relies heavily on herbs and other natural ingredients. These are often processed by baking, simmering, or roasting

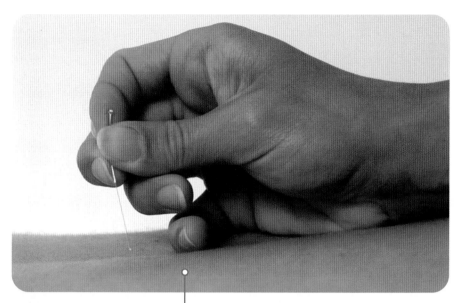

Acupuncture is a common procedure used in Chinese medicine. Acupressure is similar but practitioners use their hands not needles.

While most Chinese remedies use leaves or other parts of plants, which can be readily grown, some require animal ingredients. This brings Chinese medicine into conflict with conservationists. Rhino horns, tiger bones, and other exotic ingredients may have been common when medical preparations requiring them were first formulated, but today they are in short supply. The wild animals that produce them have been heavily hunted, sometimes to the edge of extinction. Trade in many of these animal ingredients is now banned by international law.

before being swallowed or applied directly to the affected body part.

Other types of treatment include acupuncture and moxibustion. Moxibustion involves placing fluffy leaves of a plant called *Artemisia moxa* on the skin and setting it alight. This is done to treat skin conditions.

Chinese herbal medicine is practiced in apothaceries. These are a combination of a conventional pharmacy and a doctor's office. People can either buy herbal preparations for common complaints, or, if they are unsure what is wrong with them, sit down and talk to an expert. He or she will then diagnose the problem

and prescribe a treatment. Moxibustion or acupuncture may be carried out on the spot or a particular medicine prepared to be taken home.

The Chinese have had apothaceries since the Sung Dynasty (960–1279 C.E.). A thousand years before, the Chinese had developed their own form of forensic medicine (medical techniques that produce evidence for a criminal investigation). By the Sung Dynasty, Chinese forensic medicine had become relatively advanced. Even today, the emperor Sung Tzu's book *Hsi Yuan Lu* (*A Collection of Vindicated Cases*) is considered a classic forensic text by many people involved in the field.

Chinese remedies use ingredients drawn from nature, including bark (bottom), fungus (top), and bugs, such as this centipede.

Mechanical hearts might one day be used to replace diseased ones. They would be powered by batteries.

A young cancer patient receives drug therapy in a hospital. In the future, new drugs may be able to target just cancer cells and leave healthy ones alone.

Modern medicine has had a huge impact on most people's lives. Without it, many of us would not be alive. And even those who have never been injured or seriously ill would still have to endure headaches without relief and, like it or not, live with dental cavities. Yet, despite all of the advances, there is still much that medicine cannot do. There is no cure for many cancers or AIDS (acquired immune deficiency syndrome). We also know that one or more of our organs will eventually break down and be beyond repair. Problems such as these are the challenges for medicine in the future.

A CURE FOR CANCER

One in five of all the people who die in the United States every year do so of cancer. This figure is lower than it was two decades ago, partly because of changes in lifestyles, but it is still a very significant part of the population. At the moment the only sure-fire cure for cancer is to remove the tumor and completely destroy any surviving cancerous cells. This can be done through surgery if the tumor is on the skin or in a non-essential organ such as a testicle or breast. If it is deeper inside the body, however, the surgery and follow-up treatment become more complicated and the chances of recovery decrease.

The search for a cure for cancer is currently focused on three main areas. The first of these concerns the formation of blood vessels. Tumors require new blood vessels in order to grow. Drug agents that inhibit blood vessel growth have recently been developed and these are being tested on patients in clinical trials.

The second major area of cancer research is known as gene therapy. Cancer cells form because of faults in the genetic code. Gene therapy attempts to correct these faults or bypass them by adding in new strands of DNA into affected cells. This is a very new field and progress is still in the early stages. The third approach is to develop substances known as signal blockers. If successful, these drugs would prevent the

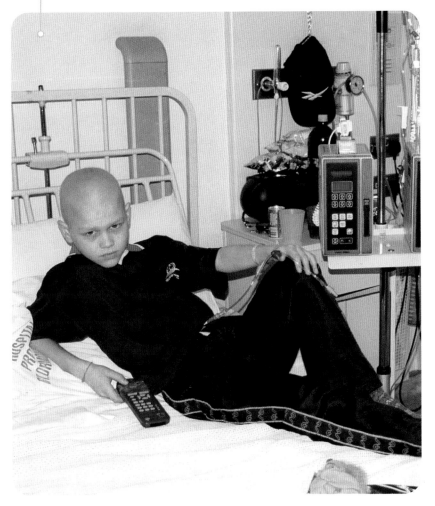

chemical reactions that cause cancer cells to grow uncontrollably into damaging tumors.

UNDERSTANDING HOW AND WHY

Aside from cures for diseases, one of the most important developments we can look forward to is greater knowledge about the environmental factors that cause them. A few decades ago, no one realized that smoking caused cancer. The effects of diet on health were also uncertain or not properly publicized. By learning more about what causes diseases, we become better able to avoid or cure them. It may be that the greatest future development in medicine is not a new drug or treatment but better understanding and education.

REPLACEMENT BODY PARTS

Heart disease is one of the world's greatest killers. It affects an essential organ, and often the only cure is to replace it with another one, through a transplant. Heart transplants have been performed successfully since 1967, but there are generally problems finding a donor, and many patients die before an organ becomes available. This problem may soon become a thing of the past. The world's first fully functioning artificial heart for transplant was devised by U.S. doctor Robert Jarvik in 1970. The first person to have one was fellow American Barney Clarke in 1982. He survived with it for 112

days. Since then, several people have had Jarvik's artificial heart transplanted. One of them lived for a full 20 months. If the design were improved, artificial hearts could become a common medical implant. They would join a growing number of replacement body parts used in surgery.

Another area where artificial implants may soon be able to help out is eyesight. Scientists have already developed a microchip that can restore vision to people that have gone blind. The microchip is placed in the retina at the back of the eyeball and the patient given glasses fitted with a charge-coupled device (CCD), similar to ones used in digital cameras. The CCD forms images of the surroundings electronically. These are then fired by laser to the microchip, which converts them into electrical signals. These are sent to the brain by nerves.

Drug researchers are currently developing foods, such as fruits or eggs, that will contain vaccines and other useful drugs. Genes that code for the required drug are added to the food by genetic engineering.

How things work

Cloning Technology

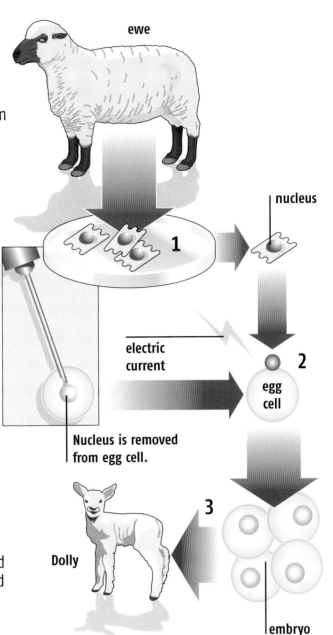

ewe

nucleus

1

electric
current

2

egg
cell

Nucleus is removed
from egg cell.

3

Dolly

embryo

Cloning is the production of an identical living copy of an animal or plant. The first ever cloned mammal was a sheep called Dolly. Dolly was born in Edinburgh, Scotland, in 1997.

In order to create Dolly, cells were taken from the udder of an adult ewe (female sheep) and grown in a laboratory (1). The udder cells then had their nuclei removed. The nucleus is where a cell's DNA is stored. Next, each nucleus was placed into another sheep's egg cell that had already had its nucleus taken out (2). Every cell in an animal, except for sex cells, contains identical DNA and identical copies of genes. (Sex cells—eggs and sperms—only have half a full set.)

The reason that adult cells look different is that most of their genes are turned "off." Only those that relate to that particular type of cell remain "on." The udder cells taken from the ewe already had most of their genes switched off, so before the process could continue the udder nuclei needed all their genes switched "on" again. This was done by passing an electric current through them, which at the same time fused the nuclei to their new surroundings.

The cells were then separated and some grew into little embryos. These were then each planted back into a ewe. Of all the embryos, one survived and it grew into Dolly (3). Dolly died in 2003, several years earlier than a normal sheep.

Dolly's creation was remarkable because she was a mammal like us. Her birth opened the way towards human cloning, which could one day have great medical value. It is illegal to clone an entire human in most places, however, doctors predict a future where cloned human cells are used to cure illness. It takes 14 days for a growing ball of human cells to begin to take on specialized roles. It is therefore impossible to tell if one cell will grow into part of a human embryo, become

the placenta, or die away completely as the new person develops. Cells like these are called stem cells. They have the potential to grow into any cell in the human body. If they could be transplanted into people suffering from otherwise untreatable diseases or injuries, these cells might be able to regenerate tissues or entire organs making them completely healthy again.

HIV AND AIDS

In 1981, a new disease was described that would change the way people lived. Acquired immune deficiency syndrome, or AIDS, caused the body's immune system to fail, leaving the sufferer defenceless against other diseases. Victims can be killed by a new infection, or develop cancers their body would normally protect them from.

AIDS is now known to be caused by a virus—the human immunodeficiency virus, or HIV for short. HIV is spread by unprotected sex, or injecting infected blood into the body. This might happen if drug users shared syringes, or if unscreened blood was used in a transfusion. In the United States, hospitals screen blood for HIV before transfusions are made. Once the virus is in the body it hides in immune system cells and cannot be gotten rid of. Untreated, it produces the symptoms of AIDS between one and ten years later.

KILLER DISEASE
Today, HIV/AIDS is the world's second most deadly contagious disease after the

Without a cure for AIDS, education about how to avoid catching the disease is the best defense against it. Here, a teacher explains the facts about the disease in a Californian classroom.

lung infection pneumonia. (A contagious disease is one that spreads directly from person to person.) According to the World Health Organization, AIDS killed more than three million people in 2002.

AIDS is currently incurable, although its symptoms can be controlled by a cocktail of drugs. About 980,000 people live with the infection in North America: 15,000 died of AIDS on the continent in 2002. Because anti-AIDS drugs are widely available in this part of the world, the quality and length of life of people infected with HIV there has improved. Many will not develop AIDS itself for decades, if at all.

In the developing world, especially Africa, anti-AIDS drugs are unavailable or too expensive. Deaths from the disease are becoming more and more common. In some parts of the continent, so many people are incapacitated by AIDS that communities cannot produce enough food for themselves.

DRUG THERAPY
To date, medical treatment can only prevent HIV from causing AIDS. Once AIDS has set in, there is nothing doctors can do to cure it. The antiviral drugs used to combat HIV are divided into reverse transcriptase inhibitors and protease inhibitors. Reverse transcriptase inhibitors alter the DNA in infected cells, which the virus needs to replicate (copy itself). They may also alter the genetic material of the virus itself. Protease inhibitors prevent the virus from producing the proteins needed for replication.

While the drugs work, they have some serious side effects, including vomiting, nausea, and diarrhea. Long-term use

> *AIDS is a major problem across the world, including Africa. Although the disease was not described until the 1980s, the first victims of the disease were Africans who died in the late 1950s.*

may lead to damage to an infected person's kidneys, liver, nerves, or eyes.

Since AIDS first appeared, more money and effort has been put into searching for a cure than any other disease. As the search for a vaccine continues, it appear that strains of HIV are becoming resistant to the antiviral drugs used to control it.

Time Line

Prehistory
Humans use wild plants to treat certain ailments.

8000 B.C.E.
Trepanning is practiced in various parts of the world. Broken bones are set with splints.

500 B.C.E.
The first hospitals appear in India.

460 B.C.E.
Hippocrates, "The Father of Modern Medicine," is born on the Greek island of Cos.

1796
In England, Edward Jenner introduces the world's first vaccine, for smallpox.

1799
Humphry Davy discovers nitrous oxide, the first anaesthetic.

PREHISTORY   500 B.C.   1500 C.E.   1800

1200 B.C.E
The concept of quarantine for infectious diseases is introduced by Israelites.

3000 B.C.E.
Sekhet'eanach practices medicine in ancient Egypt. He is history's first named physician.

1628
William Harvey determines that blood, pumped by the heart, circulates around the body.

1543
Andreas Vesalius publishes his groundbreaking textbook of anatomy, *On the Fabric of the Human Body*.

1815
René Laënnec
invents the
stethoscope.

1864
Louis Pasteur develops
germ theory of disease.

1885
Sigmund Freud develops the
technique of psychoanalysis.

1928:
Alexander Fleming
identifies penicillin,
the first antibiotic.

1978
The world's first
test-tube baby is born.

1815

1900

2000

1897
Aspirin is
developed.

1895
William Röntgen
discovers X rays.

1860
Florence
Nightingale
revolutionizes
nursing.

2003
Scientists complete
a final working
draft of the human
genome (the
complete set
of genes).

1850
The hypodermic
syringe is invented.

Glossary

addiction A mental or physical dependence on a certain chemical substance, or drug.

anesthetic A substance administered to prevent a person from feeling pain.

antibodies Blood proteins produced to counteract infectious microorganisms and other foreign substances.

arthritis Painful inflammation of the joints, usually caused by the wearing down of the connective tissue between bones.

astringent A substance that causes bleeding to stop.

dissection The cutting up of dead bodies for anatomical study.

insomnia An inability to sleep.

intravenous Directly into a vein.

ligament A band of tough, fibrous, flexible tissue linking bones together.

midwife A person qualified to deliver babies.

migraine Recurrent throbbing headache, often associated with nausea and blurred vision.

narcotic A painkilling drug that affects the workings of the brain.

nausea Sickly feeling with inclination to vomit.

nucleus The central body of an animal or plant cell, containing its DNA.

esophagus The tube leading from the back of the mouth to the stomach.

orthodontics Treatment of irregularities in the jaws and teeth.

pacemaker An electronic device that stimulates the heart and regulates heartbeat.

papyrus Paper-like material from the pithy stem of an aquatic plant.

physiologist A person who studies physiology, the science of functions of living organisms and their constituent parts.

protist A complex, single-celled organism with most of the features found in animal cells.

Renaissance A period of European history beginning in the 14th century characterized by a new spirit of enquiry into science and nature and flowering of the arts.

septic Contaminated with bacteria; festering.

shaman A village elder, wise person, or priest thought capable of communicating with spirits that are believed to cause illness.

stroke A sudden disabling attack caused by an interruption of blood flow to the brain.

tendon A tough cord of tissue connecting a muscle to a bone.

tumor A cancerous lump caused by abnormal growth of tissue.

ventilator A machine that assists breathing by controlling the flow of air into and out of the lungs.

vivisection Experimentation on a living animal.

Further Resources

Books

Medicine and Western Civilization by I. Loudon. Rutgers University Press, 2001.

Western Medicine: An Illustrated History by A. S. Lyons and J. R. Petrucelli. Oxford University Press, 1997.

The Future of Healing, Exploring the Parallels of Eastern and Western Medicine by M. P. Milburn. Crossing Press, 2001.

Web Sites

Smithsonian: Health and Human Sciences
http://www.si.edu/science_and_technology/health_and_human_sciences/

BBCi Medicine Through Time
www.bbc.co.uk/education/medicine/

Center of Disease Control and Prevention
http://www.cdc.gov/

The History of Diseases
www.mla-hhss.org/histdis.htm

Index

Page numbers in **bold** refer to feature spreads; those in *italics* refer to picture captions.

Picture Credits

Corbis: Shaen Adey; Gallo Images 81, Archivo Iconografico S.A. 17, Bettmann 8, 16, 22, 39, 46t, Bernard Bisson 35, Julian Calder 47, Louise Gubb 89, Lindsay Hebberd 80, Walter Hodges 52b, Helen King 50, Lester Lefkowitz 11, 64, 66, Roger Ressmeyer 31, 38, 54; **Getty Images**: 7, Gary Bistram 61, Chris Cheadle 70, Rita Maas 75, Gandee Vasan 86, David Young-Wolff 67; **Image State**: 68; **Imagingbody.com**: 52t, 62t, 72; **Janine Wiedel Photo Library**: 58, 62b, 69, 73; **John Foxx Images**: 2, 26, 28; **Mary Evans Picture Library**: 15; **National Library of Medicine**: 10, 12, 13, 14, 23, 25t, 25b, 41t; **PHIL**: 34, 41b, C. Goldsmith 30; **Photodisc**: 27, 29, 40, 42, 48, 49t, 49b, 56, 57, 60, 77, 83t, 83b; **Rex Features**: 55, P. Bernhard/ Fotex 74, Steve Brown 85, IPC Magazine 76, Phanie Agency 51, SIPA Press 88; **Science & Society**: Science Museum 9, 19, 36b, 46b, 71, 84; **Sylvia Cordaiy Photo Library**: 82; **Topham**: Fotomas 21, Museum of London 6, 24, Jim Pickerell/Imageworks 43, Picturepoint 18, Timothy Ross/Imageworks 36t.